From Great to Gone

From Great to Gone

Why FMCG Companies are Losing the Race for Customers

PETER LORANGE

and

JIMMI REMBISZEWSKI

Routledge
Taylor & Francis Group

LONDON AND NEW YORK

First published 2014 by Gower Publishing

Published 2016 by Routledge
2 Park Square, Milton Park, Abingdon, Oxfordshire OX14 4RN
711 Third Avenue, New York, NY 10017, USA

First issued in paperback 2016

Routledge is an imprint of the Taylor & Francis Group, an informa business

British Library Cataloguing in Publication Data
A catalogue record for this book is available from the British Library.

Library of Congress Cataloging-in-Publication Data
Lorange, Peter.
   From great to gone : why FMCG companies are losing the race for customers / by Peter
Lorange and Jimmi Rembiszewski.
      pages cm
   Includes bibliographical references and index.
   ISBN 978-1-4724-3556-9 (hardback)
1. Marketing research. 2. Consumer behavior. 3. Consumer goods. 4. New
products. 5. Strategic planning. I. Rembiszewski, Jimmi. II. Title.

   HF5415.2.L67 2014
   658.4'012--dc23

                                                                                    2013045524

ISBN 13: 978-1-138-27939-1 (pbk)
ISBN 13: 978-1-4724-3556-9 (hbk)

Contents

List of Figures and Tables

Figures

Tables

Preface and Acknowledgements

The reason for this book was very simple: it needed to be written. A monumental change among the new leading brands, in terms of global value, global consumer choice and share of consumer spending – and the impact this is having on big fast moving consumer goods (FMCG) companies – has not been covered adequately in business schools today.

The simple fact is that Apple, Google and Facebook, to name only three, have become what 20 years ago would have been called 'classic' consumer brands. And their impact on daily consumption and purchases has been one of the main reasons why Nestlé, P&G, Colgate and Unilever have to fight for a much smaller part of consumers' disposable income because they are losing their attractiveness in the hierarchy of must-have products.

So why did these newcomers become great? What did they do differently from the classic FMCGs? And why did the former greats not change their business models?

In this book, we try to provide some answers and give examples of companies and products that have maintained their status of greatness during the new century.

The key is the ability of these companies to innovate fast and via a more integrated communication/supply chain approach. They deliver to consumers rapidly and credibly, replacing lengthy and indirect value claims. This allows this new breed of companies direct consumer contact and total control of their products and brands throughout the production, retail and delivery process – all touch points between manufacture and consumer that allow for dialogue.

Speed of innovation and control of the value chain is the key to success in the twenty-first century. Otherwise, companies will end up in what we term the 'innovation gap' (too long a time between innovations). This leads to the arrival of lower-priced, me-too, generic products and value propositions, all resulting in lower margins. This squeezed margin and increasing value offers are what most FMCGs face today and it is most pronounced in the mature and saturated markets of North America and Europe.

In the recent past, even many of the 'great' companies and brands that we analyse in this book have fallen into this innovation gap – moving from 'great' to 'good', the process we capture in the title of this book. Apple, Nokia and even Nespresso seem to have found themselves in this position and like the old FMCGs before them are reacting with old-fashioned TV advertising and promotion and bringing out lower-priced variations of their own products. They too seem to act rather defensively, losing sight of what made them great in the first place, that is, a fast innovation pipeline with an outstanding route to market (delivery) concept.

One of the key observations in this book is that a major obstacle to faster innovation is inflexible marketing and established brand strategies. These seem to prevent a lot of companies from looking beyond the core benefits of their products for new ideas. Our suggestion is to replace these well-crafted strategies with a sort of building blocks ('Lego') strategy that will allow more flexibility to innovate and give consumers the opportunity to construct what they want their individual brand experience to be.

We intend this book to provoke a rethink and debate about a new marketing model. It is meant for two main audiences. First, enlightened business executives who want to prepare themselves more thoroughly for the revolution that is about to take place in several sectors of the business world – a more networked reality where the strength of economies no longer seems so critical. What matters more is to develop a combined understanding of modern consumers, how to pull off innovations that they appreciate and how to communicate these innovations to them in a relevant and contemporary way. As well as executives working in FMCG businesses, there is a much broader potential audience for this book, including luxury goods, business to business (b2b) businesses, banking and insurance. Even the public sector can take lessons from what we have to say.

Second, this book can serve as a text for advanced students (Executive MBA and executive education programme participants) who are studying the interface between modern consumer behaviour, innovation theory and communication. While many undergraduate business programmes run these as three separate courses, we contend that they should be treated as one.

Finally, we recommend this book to all enlightened readers who want to prepare themselves more thoroughly for the silent revolution that is about to reshape much of our society – a radically different model from economic value creation, with innovation, not traditional cost-cutting, at its centre.

Acknowledgements

We are indebted to too many from both the business and academic worlds – former executive colleagues and former students – to acknowledge all individually here. They know who they are and their input is highly valued. Eight senior executives have made specific contributions to this book: Renée Bernhard, President, Bernhard Company; Patrice Bula, SVP, Nestlé; Herbert Hainer, CEO, Adidas; Ken Levy, Executive Director, G2 Worldwide; Rahul Prakash, former Head of Global Trade Marketing and Distribution, BAT Canada; Gian Peiro Beghelli, CEO, Beghelli; Gerry Wang, CEO, Seaspan; and Jorgen Vig Knudsdorp, CEO, Lego. We gratefully acknowledge and thank them for their invaluable insights and contributions.

We also want to give our sincere thanks to Andrea Zlobinski for guiding us along the way and her excellent administrative support. Sally Simmons of Cambridge Editorial has edited the various drafts of the book with strong commitment and an impressive professional bent. Without Sally, and the support of her colleagues Kate Kirk and David C. Taylor, this book would not have become a reality. Finally, we wish to thank Jonathan Norman and the team at Gower Publishing for their encouragement. In the end, however, it is the authors who share the responsibility for what is presented in this book.

Introduction

From Great to Gone

We chose the title of this book – *From Great to Gone* – very deliberately. It obviously alludes to Jim Collins' classic *Good To Great*,[1] which discussed how companies in the twentieth century built organisations and business models that truly made them the envy of the world.

Among them were all the top FMCGs and their global brands. These global brands also dominated the league tables of the top 20 most valuable brands for a large part of the last century. They included household names like Marlboro, Colgate, Gillette, General Foods, Douwe Egberts, Ferrero, Mars, Pepsi, Sony, Shell, Henkel, Nivea, C&A, as well as high street banks and top auto brands.

Only a decade later, ten years or so into the new millennium, we see that most of these 'great' corporations are no longer dominant and their key brands hardly make the list of the top ten most valuable global brands. Even worse, some of the companies themselves have ceased to exist, for example, General Foods and Gillette.

What happened? Why did they not master the start of the twenty-first century, when they had everything going for them – global awareness of their brands, deep pockets, presence in a world of unprecedented free access and a great corporate attractiveness among the worldwide talent pool?

The single answer is that they did not see how radically the twenty-first century consumer has changed. The e-revolution has not only brought changes in the communication landscape but, more importantly, a new consumer who requires a total transformation of the current business model. The relatively simple brand strategies of the twentieth century, basically following the proven P&G marketing approach together with a route to market built nearly 100 years ago, have become outdated.

---

1   Collins, J. (2001) *Good to Great: Why Some Companies Make the Leap … and Others Don't*, New York, Random House.

Table I.1   Top ten global brands 2000 and 2012

	2000	2012
1	Coca-Cola	Coca-Cola
2	Microsoft	Apple
3	IBM	IBM
4	Intel	Google
5	Nokia	Microsoft
6	GE	GE
7	Ford	McDonald's
8	Disney	Intel
9	McDonald's	Samsung
10	AT&T	Toyota

Note: Apple and Google sat well outside the top 20 in 2000; in 2012 they were among the top five.

These outdated business models and their global organisations cannot meet the need for a radical, innovation-based business platform that delivers much faster product cycles stimulated by a new breed of consumer, who is used to these cycles from modern e-products.

The clear winners of the twenty-first century are not the great FMCGs but companies that can deliver new consumer products fast. Hence this book calls for a transformation from FMCGs – fast moving consumer goods – to FICGs – fast *innovating* consumer goods companies.

It is mainly the new e-commerce players that have moved from good to great (see Table I.1). Google, Apple, Facebook and Amazon are the leaders in today's corporate and brand rankings. This is also reflected in the meteoritic rise in their valuation. It is also strange that senior managers of old-fashioned FMCGs do not see these companies as real competitors, despite the fact that their products have cut a significant slice out of the disposable income of the new consumer. The traditional consumer goods brands now have to fight extremely hard for a much smaller piece of the cake. While mobile phones and computers were previously seen as investment product categories, as opposed to everyday consumer goods, the effect of SMS, emails, apps, photos and social networking sites generates a daily outlay. One of the key learnings of this book is that P&G, Nestlé, Colgate and Unilever must regard Google, Apple and Facebook as competition for the daily consumer spend.

Table I.2   Biggest growth in brand value – the top ten brands (2011)[2]

Position	Company	% growth
1	Apple	58%
2	Amazon.com	32%
3	Google	27%
4	Samsung	20%
5	Burberry	20%
6	Hyundai	19%
7	Caterpillar	19%
8	Cartier	18%
9	Oracle	16%
10	eBay	16%

Note the presence of three internet-based companies and two luxury goods companies in this ranking.

One might speculate that this is only a phenomenon in countries where the disposable income is fairly limited. However, we see the same thing across the globe with the biggest impact in North America and Europe. These are the markets in which the traditional FMCGs suffer most. Their inability to compete with faster innovation cycles has led to an *innovation gap* which, as we show in this book, leads directly to pricing pressure and low margins.

It might seem counterintuitive but it is not only the new age companies that have coped well with the new consumer; some of the oldest luxury label corporations, such as Cartier, Hermès and Gucci, are doing better than ever (Table I.2). We will show that their ability to innovate fast and deliver these innovations very effectively to the marketplace has enabled them to move from good to great in the twenty-first century.

We also discuss the key obstacles traditional FMCGs face when competing in this new environment. We cover brand strategies, marketing organisations, R&D set-ups, route to market strategies, slow decision making and outdated organisation principles. For some of these we will give examples of how they could be transformed. However, we believe that it is too early to assess the full spectrum of the changes we have seen over the past decade on twenty-first century marketing strategies. As former Chinese premier Zhou Enlai is reputed

---

2   *The Times*, 5 October 2011, p. 43.

to have said, when questioned about the legacy of the French Revolution, for the wider implications of these changes, 'It's much too soon to tell.'

This is a book for senior managers in FMCGs and management consultancies – and for anyone with a general interest in consumer change or more particularly marketing theory, including professionals in industries that face a consumer challenge and where global recipes are no longer feeding a global marketplace. It will also present some stimulating challenges for academic economists, psychologists and anthropologists. Throughout the book, we use case study examples from a wide range of companies across different sectors to illustrate good and bad practice and support our ideas.

Chapter 1

The Dilemmas of FMCGs in the Twenty-first Century

This book is overdue. We are more than a decade into the third millennium and enough time has passed for us to be able to assess the consequences of a seismic shift in the behaviour and quality of twenty-first-century consumers and the impact they have had on the industries that sell to them every day. As we shall see, the modern consumer's familiarity with multimedia communications technology has played a key role in bringing this change about.

Many of the current problems for FMCGs seem to us to be inextricably linked to a major theme in this book, which is that companies do not innovate; or if they do innovate, they do not do it in the right way. The old world, and the lumbering FMCG giants that have been used to ruling it, are slowly dying. The economic environment has taken a major blow and it is now a question of adapt or die. Too often, the only response of these classic premier league FMCG companies to the changing economic climate is to cut costs.

The environment presents FMCGs with numerous dilemmas; for some we can provide guidance, others will be solved only through experience and learning and still others we can do little more than identify. For example, there is the dilemma of the effect of corporate governance on creativity. Corporate governance is in many ways poison to the creative and innovation processes within a company and it is easy to get to the point where the board is more preoccupied with risk management and covering its back than it is with building the top line. Another dilemma is how to find a sustainable way to give the people in middle and lower management opportunities to make strategic decisions – because without that opportunity they will never grow. Yet here we run into the problem of control. On the one hand there are a few companies, like Apple for example, which have strong direction from the top yet manage to allow innovation at all levels; while on the other hand most big

> 'The old world, and the lumbering FMCG giants that have been used to ruling it, are slowly dying.'

companies also want to grow their people yet have stringent control mechanisms that suppress creativity. They find control and innovation difficult to reconcile.

'There has been a fundamental change in consumers and consumer behaviour for which FMCGs have not calculated.'

There are no quick or easy answers to dilemmas like these. A winning company needs to have people at the top who have both the guts to lead and the ability to stimulate all the way down through the organisation. This is an art and it's not obvious how it can be managed sustainably.

This has been driven by three main factors:

The first is the cyberworld, which has supplied new forms of communication, unlimited global accessibility, new sorts of data, instant feedback, boundless dialogue and enhanced transparency through easy access to information. The cyberworld has blown apart Maslow's hierarchy of needs as it applies to human motivation in the modern consumer goods market. Today's 18–20 year olds *must have* the means and ability to connect and communicate – in particular, access to the internet. This is now top of the hierarchy. The new consumers are experts at handling the new media, which are quantitative (giving us more, all the time, and faster) rather than qualitative (being very low on literature). But the crucial point is that consumer behaviour has changed because consumers themselves have changed.

There is a new consumer emerging, one who was born 20 years ago and who now represents the most important purchasing group in the world. These new consumers are typically relatively young multitaskers; they move seamlessly between swiping their iPad or iPhone, working on their laptop and watching a TV programme or film they are streaming, and occasionally talking to each other. What might seem a media and informational overload to their seniors – not to mention rude behaviour – seems perfectly natural to them. These are the people who are the true drivers for growth in FMCG companies and they are attracted to prestige (through branding), newness, speed and quality rather than lower prices.

These consumers decide everything and that poses huge marketing challenges. They use the media as a meeting place and are comfortable with an unprecedented intensity of interaction and dialogue. They are intelligent but many of them are disaffected because they are embarking on their working lives surrounded by the fallout from a global recession of unprecedented severity. Jobs are scarce and those who seem to have all the power and wealth – for example, bankers and politicians from a previous generation – are despised as greedy and corrupt. These young consumers are cynical before their time. They want change, they value innovation and they know they have a voice; they are almost impossible to reach through traditional marketing routes. There is a disconnect between older marketers and young consumers; it is very difficult for traditional marketers, who are used to putting consumers into categories, and creates a level of organisational stress.

The second factor driving change is the speed of innovation. Technological progress has accelerated to a degree that consumers now expect new, better products hitting the shelves every six months – and for minimal extra cost. Because many FMCGs are not capable of this rate of innovation, expectations have adjusted and now all FMCGs must strive to deliver.

'Technological progress has accelerated to a degree that consumers now expect new, better products hitting the shelves every six months.'

Nestlé has developed a six-point programme to train young executives to develop and keep a competitive advantage as the leading nutrition, health and wellness provider in the world. The aim is to develop edge through relevant innovations, including:

- Making choices. This implies saying no to some projects and pursuing only relevant innovations.

- Grasping opportunities and pursuing them aggressively.

- Valuing what consumers value. This means understanding the key preferences of the modern consumer and coming up with innovations that they will appreciate and understand.

- Engaging with the community and stakeholders.

- Communicating through the right media. Innovations need to be communicated effectively and digital means are the way today rather than traditional advertising.

- Having the best people. This is an essential condition for achieving this innovation-centred agenda.

The third factor is the cost of servicing this fast-developing communications technology. Mobile telephony, social networking and instant communications have had a massive effect on the amount of money available for traditional consumer goods, many of which have lost some of their allure and come under enormous spending pressure, driving prices down. A telephone was originally seen as an investment product – you'd expect to buy one, maybe two, in a lifetime. But mobile phones have shown themselves to be consumer products. The speed at which communications technology has been taken over our lives is unprecedented in the history of mankind – as witnessed in the developed world where a significant percentage of disposable income now goes on products and services that didn't exist 20 years ago. Even Nokia, initially one of the leaders in mobile telephony, underestimated its effect, predicting ten years ago that it would have tens of millions of customers; in fact it has billions.

Even more surprising than the extent to which mobile telephony has revolutionised consumer spending in the developed world is the way in which it has managed to take root in the world's poorest continent: Africa. In most of sub-Saharan Africa (as well as eastern Europe and south-east Asia) electronic technology is expensive, often unreliable and invariably the preserve only of the wealthiest in society. Mobile phones are the exception. In less than 15 years they have become ubiquitous – in Uganda alone, it is estimated that about a third of the population owns a mobile phone and the number is growing. This is true throughout Africa: in 1998 there were fewer than four million mobile phones in the continent; today it's more like half a billion.

Nor is it just the number of phones in circulation that is remarkable. It is also the way in which the technology has been harnessed to serve the peculiar requirements of developing countries. In a continent renowned for its death-trap roads, sparse rail networks and intermittent power grids, mobile phones are one way of overcoming the region's enormous communications problems. Mobile telephony has helped big businesses operate more efficiently, but more importantly it has opened up huge opportunities for the hundreds of thousands of small businesses on which African economies all depend. Not only can farmers and fishermen now check market prices quickly and get a decent price for their produce, but anybody can now use a mobile phone to make and receive payments – an application that has largely been ignored by the rest of the world.

Mobile telephony is also revolutionising the way companies reach their customers. For example, in Asian markets mobile devices are increasingly becoming the first and often the only way for people to access banking services. While mobile access is a helpful optional add-on for western customers, it has become a critical success factor for banks wanting to establish themselves in countries where potential customers would otherwise have to walk miles to reach a branch. In these markets, banks have leap-frogged the classic evolutionary pathway to attracting customers: 'They don't have the legacy systems and practices to overcome. They can skip the branch build-out and capture customers straight on to the state-of-the-art platforms.'[1]

More generally, social scientists now have access to huge amounts of data derived from mobile phone records and social networking sites that can enable them to pinpoint and predict people's behaviour with extraordinary accuracy: 'Song Chaoming … a reasearcher at Northeastern University in Boston … has devised an alogorithm which can look at someone's mobile phone records and predict with an average of 93 per cent accuracy where that person is at any given moment of the day … [H]is accuracy was never lower than 80 per cent for any of the 50,000 people he looked at.'[2] It is not difficult to see how companies applying the same methods could gain unparalleled access to information about their customers' purchasing intentions.

So the phenomenal rise of mobile phone technology, with its ability to connect huge and complex social networks, instantly, across the entire globe, has changed the consumer. How have the marketers responded?

> *'The FMCG sector has failed to realise that its lunch has been eaten.'*

We believe that most of the traditional FMCG sector has been getting it wrong. It has failed to recognise that its lunch has been eaten and has not responded to these challenges, for two main reasons. The first is that it didn't see this technology as a game changer. It viewed the change in consumer behaviour as a trend that would modify its communications and its use of media but it did not see the underlying structural problems. Consumers are spending their money elsewhere. Today, the key competition for P&G, Unilever, Nestlé and Colgate are technology companies like Apple and Facebook, which have a far more profound effect on young consumer spending than any product in their traditional categories and are now seen as fast-moving consumer products. Established companies are losing their share of new business and having to compete for the money in the consumer's purse. Pricing pressure has forced the FMCG sector into a position where profit margins are getting progressively narrower while the consumer goods they sell are becoming increasingly difficult to differentiate on quality. We will argue in Chapter 3 that this is

---

1   Davies, P.J. (2013) 'Banking's handy revolution', *Financial Times*, 28 February.
2   *The Economist* (2013) 'Dr Seldon, I presume', 23 February, p. 68.

the real innovation gap that FMCGs face – the gap between the traditional innovation cycle of years and the new innovation cycle that customers now expect, a matter of months before new products are launched. When companies fall into this innovation gap, profit margins fall. The second reason that the FMCG sector got it so wrong is that it is hampered by internal and external barriers to innovation, as we will examine in detail in Chapters 4 and 5.

> 'Today, the key competition for P&G, Unilever and Colgate are technology companies like Apple and Facebook.'

Further factors are changes in distribution and identifying where growth is going to come from. New ways of communicating and bonding with the consumer have led to a very different role for distribution. For example, the clothing company Burberry, based in Knightsbridge in London, uses Twitter-based communication with its customers to determine what they are interested in and the store is stocked accordingly.

In times of economic turbulence a more intense focus on one stakeholder group – the customers – seems to be warranted. This will stimulate further growth, either directly, by securing more top-line growth (sales), or indirectly, by creating a more realistic basis for sustainable bottom-line growth (profits). More than ever, the customer is king. We can no longer stick to a balanced scorecard approach, which would call for focusing more or less equally on several stakeholder groups, as prescribed by Kaplan and Norton.[3] Instead, we have to make sure we get as close as possible to one key stakeholder group, the customers.

In a recent series of TV interviews on CNN (7 March 2013) several prominent CEOs (of Adidas, Daimler and Bayer) emphasised the critical importance of top-line growth in markets in the US, China and Russia, rather than in the European markets with which they are more familiar. All three stressed the importance of being aligned with the geographic markets that have the best propensity for top-line growth. But this implies, of course, that companies need to understand their customers in each of these specific markets, and that innovations relevant to each are implemented and communicated.

This might sound obvious to the point of being glib but we have very recently seen how even the most successful companies can get this badly wrong. On 17 April 2013, the UK-based retail giant Tesco announced that it was pulling out of the US, following the company's first fall in annual profits in 20 years.

---

3   Kaplan, R.S. and Norton, D.P. (1996) *The Balanced Scorecard*, Harvard Business School Press.

Six years earlier, Tesco had launched its chain of budget grocery stores, Fresh & Easy, in the US. The venture had struggled from the start in the market, where it pitched itself against Trader Joe's, an established chain also owned by a major European retail group, Aldi. Both stores stock limited lines of own-brand items and both aim to provide good-quality, wholesome food at lower prices. Yet Trader Joe's has thrived, while Tesco is withdrawing from Fresh & Easy at an estimated loss of £1.2 billion. Why?

Tesco chief executive Philip Clarke pointed to the part played by technology and changes in shopping habits: 'The world is so different now from 2004–5 when the research was originally undertaken – who was shopping on a smart phone back then? In fact, who owned a smart phone back then?'[4]

However, Emma Vickers, writing in *The Guardian*,[5] identifies other reasons, not least Tesco's failure to understand customers' needs and preferences: 'The key difference between the two lies in Trader Joe's focus on customer experience – the cheery staff wear Hawaiian shirts, morning shoppers get free coffee and kids get rolls of stickers. Over at Fresh & Easy, customers fend for themselves at self-service checkouts.'

Tesco in the US fell into a yawning innovation gap: despite its extensive research, it managed to enter the most competitive market in the US without an edge; it brought nothing new to the US; it went in on a totally wrong premise (that the US would readily adopt the UK's self-service, budget goods model); and it failed to leverage one of its most valuable assets – its name.

Stories like this underline the importance of understanding key customers and we should be asking ourselves some basic questions: Who are they? Are new groups of key customers emerging? How do they prefer to be served? There the answer seems to be relevant – and rapid – innovations. And how do we communicate these innovations to the target customers? If we can handle these three steps successfully – identifying and understanding today's key customers, coming up with effective innovations to meet their needs and communicating these innovations effectively – we might be able to see more top-line growth at higher prices (that is, bottom-line growth, higher margins).

---

4   *Metro* (2013) 'Tesco confirms US exit as annual profits fall', 17 April.
5   *The Guardian* (2013) 'Tesco expected to scrap struggling US grocery chain Fresh & Easy', 12 April.

As a consequence of these factors, we believe that the classic FMCG leviathans have to change radically, not only in terms of their communication and media strategies, but also in their marketing and brand strategies, innovation set-up and innovation cycles. They are hampered by their sheer size and they need to develop a new route to market. Otherwise the innovation gap will mean that they face permanent pricing pressure coupled with decline which will lead to lower margins and unsustainably low profit growth. This cycle will bring these modern dinosaurs to extinction if they don't change their ways.

Unfortunately, at the moment the old received wisdom still holds sway in the world of marketing. FMCGs are still seen as the gold standard when it comes to getting close to the consumer and they are still seen as the quintessential training ground for each new generation of marketers. This should no longer be the case – as a closer look at the mobile phone industry reveals. Far from being a history of technological innovations pushed at the consumer in the traditional way, the history of the mobile phone has so far been a chronicle of consumer engagement and changes in consumer habits, allowing mobile phones to take on different roles as they developed in line with customer needs.

Handheld mobile phones as we know them first appeared following the introduction of cellular networks in the early 1980s. These networks employed a series of receiver–transmitter towers located at the nodes of a network made up of hexagonal cells. Each tower was designed to receive and transmit signals in three directions, enabling communication across the entire network and hence over long distances. Before the introduction of cellular networks, 'mobile' telephones (which usually comprised a number of components, including the handset, mounted permanently inside a vehicle) could only be called via an operator who had to identify the nearest base station to the phone before connecting the call. By the late 1980s, cellular networks were springing up in the US, Europe and Japan and the practicality of a genuinely mobile telephone became a reality. The Nordic countries – Denmark, Finland, Norway and Sweden – were notable pioneers, with the Nordic Mobile Telephone (NMT) system being launched in 1983, giving industrial companies such as Ericsson and Nokia an early lead. But these companies were infrastructure-focused: they were not FMCGs.

Emerging as they did during the boom years of the 1980s, mobile phones quickly became (along with the Porsche 911 and the now quaintly old-fashioned Filofax personal organiser) a staple accessory for the new breed of young, upwardly mobile professionals – the 'yuppies'. Actor Michael Douglas's portrayal of fictional corporate raider Gordon Gekko in the award-winning 1987 and 2010 films *Wall Street* and *Wall Street: Money Never Sleeps* firmly established the mobile phone (in this case a Motorola DynaTAC handset the size of a brick) as the ultimate symbol of power and status. From about 1990 onwards, the mobile phone has continued its upward trajectory, becoming ever more sophisticated and capable. By the end of the twentieth century the novelty had worn off and the mobile phone had become an indispensable tool. But by then, it was fast becoming the single most influential connection between the marketer and the consumer. It provided instant and targeted messaging – in both directions: it was interactive. Pretty soon, public payphones fell into disuse and many households dispensed with a fixed landline.

In the mid-1990s, the convergence of two developing technologies resulted in the camera phone, an otherwise arbitrary combination of functions, but one that proved decisive in the evolution of the device. Although the camera phone resulted from introducing a camera function for a mobile phone, the original idea was the reverse – that is, to build communications capability into a camera. A number of patents exist for such devices dating back as far as 1956. French-born inventor and entrepreneur Philippe Kahn is credited with having taken the first digital photograph (of his new-born daughter) with a camera phone and instantly sharing it over a public network via a mobile phone. That was in 1997. As with many new inventions – especially those designed to be carried and used by human hands – miniaturisation was the focus of early mobile phone developers. To be truly portable, the phone has to be small enough and light enough to be carried easily in a jacket or trouser pocket. Devices like Gordon Gekko's Motorolla DynaTAC were clearly too big.

Size and price reduction was relatively easy to achieve and within ten years of its appearance on the market, the mobile phone had gone from being a 1kg metal and plastic brick to being a tiny bauble not much bigger than a cigarette lighter. Interestingly, this trend had gone too far to accommodate the next phase of

> 'Mobile phone development led, and was led by, the consumer.'

technological development. As mobile phones became more capable, internet browsing and email capability were added. That meant a larger screen with better picture resolution was needed. The smallest phones were now too small to make use of this new requirement. Screens got bigger and – in order to avoid making the entire device too big again – touch-screen technology was included so as to dispense with the need for a keypad. The smart phone was born.

Throughout this rapid evolution, consumer expectation and technological innovation advanced in tandem. No sooner had an engineer or designer voiced a new capability than a consumer or industry pundit found an application – how else could the camera phone have become reality? No conventional marketer would have countenanced such an arbitrary marriage. Thus mobile phone development led, and was led by, the consumer. With internet connectivity now available, designers were able to extend the versatility of the smart phone to an unprecedented extent. Throughout the 30 years since the first mobile phones appeared, processing power had continually increased, batteries had steadily become smaller, more powerful and longer lasting, and the internet had blossomed into the primary communications medium for business and private use.

Social networking via websites like Facebook, YouTube and Myspace was immediately exploited by mobile telephony. And the advent of mobile phone applications – apps – made smart phones the electronic equivalent of the multi-purpose Swiss Army knife. Suddenly consumers had a handheld device that could be used for fact-finding about product features, instant research into consumer feedback, and from the manufacturers' side directed advertising and information distribution.

This in turn has led to the development of the tablet computer, a machine that combines the functions (including a touch-sensitive qwerty keyboard that can be changed for four different European languages at the touch of a button) and processing power of a laptop computer with the versatility and interactivity of the smart phone.

Thirty years is not a long time in the evolution of most inventions but mobile phones are one notable exception. The result of a remarkable combination of technological breakthroughs – microprocessors, digital imaging, battery power, the creation of the worldwide web and development of social networking and media sharing, even GSM satellite navigation – the mobile phone is the one device that has been able to exploit them all. Today, industries and businesses cannot ignore the power of the mobile phone. It is arguably the most powerful communications medium – at least in the developed world – and possibly the most important marketing tool since the invention of the newspaper advertisement or TV advertising.

With any new technology, the 'early adopters' are always a defining force in its subsequent development. The interesting thing about the mobile phone industry is that, even now, nearly all consumers are still 'early adopters' if

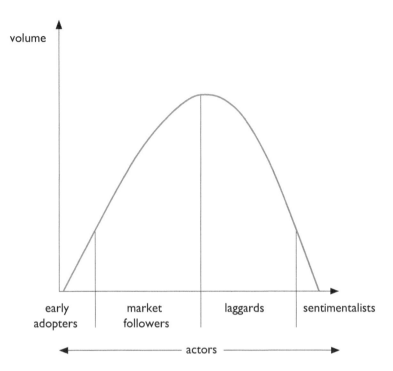

Figure 1.1   **The classic growth curve for a successful new product or service**

only by virtue of the fact that a new generation of phone seems to appear every other year. The classic growth curve for a successful new product or service is illustrated in Figure 1.1. You will see that the sales development of the new product or service follows a classic bell-shaped curve: take-off, growth, decline and ultimately phase-out. For some new products or services the path of this curve might be very steep – consumer electronics, for instance, typically follows such a rapid evolution. At the other extreme we might find certain products that have become part of our daily life and after reaching a plateau, remain there for years or even generations. For example, we have worked with a well-known drinks brand (now a part of a much larger global group), which claims that its best-known brand – a popular liqueur – is the same today as it was over 100 years ago. It shows no sign of going out of fashion. Even more extreme, the Roman Catholic Church is reputed to be the oldest organisation in the world still in existence, and the service offered by this institution appears to follow a life-cycle curve of extreme length.

And we also see from Figure 1.1 that the development of this life-cycle is driven by various different consumer groups:

- The early adoptors – these are open to innovations; they are trendsetters and influencers of others. They like to take risks.

- Market followers – these are open to innovations but they must be convinced that the new approach works; they keep a close eye on the early adopters.

- Laggards – these are slow to pick up on new products. They may be traditionalists, satisfied with the status quo, or simply lazy. They only adopt when the evidence of the added benefits from the new approach is overwhelming.

- The sentimentalists – these adopt when it is more or less all over. This group might be seen as clinging to the by-now established approach in a nostalgic way.

All these consumer groups have important roles to play but none more so than the early adopters who, after all, are the ones who set the whole process in motion. The early adopters always look for something new, something better. Although typically well-served by existing products, they are always receptive to new ideas by which we usually mean rapid but small, incremental, improvements rather than major leaps forward. These early adopters are often the younger generation who are looking for innovations that can help them become more efficient multi-taskers by building upon what they already know and have. Today, these early adopters are invariably active users of social media. For them the worldwide web is familiar territory and the context for much of their social, commercial and business activity. Not for these people the traditional medium of television or newspaper ads; not for them the classic point-of-sale promotional literature. Instead word of mouth (metaphorically, as it is usually via the medium of a handheld electronic device) plays a key role.

'Brand loyalty is always conditional upon the provider's ability to innovate, evolve and – most importantly – interact with the customer.'

The challenge for corporations is to maintain a close bond with the early adopters for whom brand loyalty, though often fierce, is always conditional upon the provider's ability to innovate, evolve and – most importantly – interact with the customer. The product or service provider must be so completely in touch with its customers that it not only knows what other headline brands the customer favours, but can second-guess each phase in the evolution of the customer's lifestyle expectations.

A key capability is to have new products and services ready to launch long before the existing product's life-cycle is complete. Novelty is crucial. This is illustrated in Figure 1.2, which shows a wave-shaped set of product life-cycles building on each other. To achieve this is often easier said than done – it is typically not a small task to figure out the 'next generation', and for several reasons: first, the early adopters group may be changing. Do we still understand who these consumers are? The generation of early adopters that embraced the personal computer is not the same as today's multi-taskers who manage their lives with an iPhone. Second, the technological innovative response may be wrong. When consumer expectation evolves at about the same speed as product innovation, there is always the risk that the product developer will misjudge the next step and in so doing lose ground to a competitor. In the mobile phone sector, Nokia, for instance, focused on better phone functionality and smaller phones at a time when Apple chose ease of use combined with a multitude of novel functions. Apple came out as the winner and Nokia has never been able to reconnect with the early adopters despite having produced excellent and innovative products since then.

In pre-empting consumer preferences, having a portfolio of products to play on is essential. Looking again at Apple, we see that this company consistently comes up with new products that appeal to early adopters. Ease of use is a consistent theme. Appealing design is another. Understanding of the user's psychology is yet another and probably more elusive element – Apple understood before most of its rivals that swiping a touch-screen is psychologically more appealing than pushing buttons. Thus Apple has managed to keep ahead of the competition with its iPod, iPhone and iPad products. The result is the wave-shaped growth curve of Figure 1.2.

Another key factor in achieving the sort of wave-type growth shown here is the ability to shorten the tail end of the typical bell-shaped trajectory (Figure 1.1). Companies such as Apple, H&M and Zara can introduce innovative new products and more or less 'force' the existing product offering into obsolescence because they have their own stores. These companies can observe more effectively how the new products perform in their own stores, making relatively rapid changes to the products and even withdrawing unsuccessful products with little risk of loss. Developing mechanisms such as this to monitor the effects of innovation in a controlled way is becoming essential.

When the mobile phone industry started out it was focused on satisfying a core consumer need to be able to communicate with others whenever they wanted, wherever they were. In the early phases companies concentrated

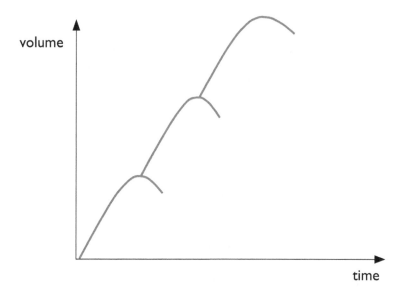

Figure 1.2   A wave-shaped set of product life-cycles

on bringing in consumers through ever more accessible offers. And in that they have been immensely successful. Mobile telephony has captured more disposable consumer income in a shorter period of time than any new product category in history.

The mobile phone companies probably expected to improve and innovate on what could be seen as the key end benefit: better voice-based communication. That would have been the classic FMCG way, leading to market saturation and price wars. Indeed, as we all know, prices for basic mobile phones and calls tumbled rapidly, leading to brutal fights for market share and margin erosion. But then something else happened: companies started moving into innovations that the old model would have denounced as off-strategy. The built-in camera, for example.

'The move from voice communication to visual communication is as radical as if a Mars bar played music as you bit into it.'

Imagine the scene at the board presentation: your company has spent trillions building up its networks, buying licences in all major countries and setting up infrastructure to *sell phones*. Then someone asks the board to let them develop a phone with a camera in it. Under the old traditional model, the idea would have died right there – as would the career of the off-message upstart who had suggested it. Nevertheless, someone did just that and nowadays every mobile phone has a camera – and not just a camera but a feature that allows you to record high-quality still images or video anywhere and send them as an attachment via email or download them onto a computer where they can be digitally stored and manipulated. This move from voice communication to visual communication is as radical as if a Mars bar played music as you bit into it. Such innovations created new, off-strategy income streams within the product category. And, surprisingly, the advent of the smart phone has not had a major impact on sales of digital cameras as had been feared. Only sales of low-end cameras, with image quality no better than the equivalent phone, have been affected. Sales of high-end cameras have actually increased as people become turned on to photography. The newest cameras to be developed are even incorporating some of the advantages of mobile technology – including Wifi and GPS.

Developing your product in parallel with consumer preferences – shadowing them and occasionally pre-empting them rather than following the consumer reactively – is a prerequisite of product marketing in today's world. The closer you are to your consumer, the easier this is and the more you can learn about their other product preferences.

However, simply aligning yourself with your customers is not enough. You must think like them, interact like them and indeed interact *with* them as individuals: you must get every single one of them to buy into your brand but at the same time you must treat every single one of them independently. Social media are the key and technology is the means. Burberry has proved itself very smart in this respect, being one of the first corporations to launch its own Facebook page (which quickly attracted over half a million 'friends') before launching its own exclusive social networking site, artofthetrench.com. Although it still maintains its own stores and still places print ads in the fashion glossies, Burberry relies far more today on social networking to spread the word and bring in new customers. Indeed, the 'exclusivity' of artofthetrench.com has made is all the more desirable even though, paradoxically, it's not in the least exclusive – anybody can sign up. Another social media platform, Twitter, has helped Burberry to establish its vast store in downtown Shanghai, its toe-hold in China. Burberry uses Twitter to promote its products to Chinese consumers and stocks its mega-store based on the feedback it receives.

> 'You must think like your customers, interact like them and indeed interact with them as individuals.'

UK-based drinks giant Diageo, a classic FMCG company which owns brands such as Guinness, Johnny Walker, Smirnoff and Baileys, has found another way to cosy up to the Chinese consumer. The Diageo approach to the Chinese market is more extreme than Burberry's, opening an exclusive store or 'private house' in Beijing that caters to the super-rich and offers personalised blends of Scotch whisky costing thousands of dollars per bottle. Other luxury brands have taken a similar approach; Gucci can no longer sell its trademark brown logo bags in China – they have become too ubiquitous – so the company now markets personalised rare skin bags that cannot be found in Europe or America. In fact many brands have 'Chinesified' their products to such an extent that European and American consumers would neither recognise them nor choose to buy them: Mont Blanc sells pens adorned with Chinese dragons and the stylish and sedate Rolls-Royce produced a $1 million China-only 'Year of the Dragon' version of the Phantom, with hand-painted red dragons along the sides and dragons hand-embroidered on the upholstery. Swiss upper-end jeweller and watchmaker Chopard has an annual turnover of more than €500 million, out of which its luxury watches, known for its restrained styling, account for slightly less than half. The company now produces more flamboyant jewellery specifically for its Chinese customers. The co-CEO of Chopard, Karl-Friedrich Scheufele, states that his firm's success is due to two principal factors – a focus on innovations and new designs and rapid expansion in Asia, particularly through wholly-owned stores.

> 'To exploit an emerging market you must learn what the consumer wants, latch onto it immediately and then go on a journey with the customers as they evolve.'

What all these companies have realised is that different customers need different treatment. To exploit an emerging market you must learn what the consumer wants, latch onto it immediately and then go on a journey with the customers as they evolve. Naturally, a lot depends upon absolute wealth and disposable income. China is quickly becoming wealthier whereas consumers in other emerging markets remain relatively poor. Companies targeting Africa, for example, are taking a very different approach to one they would adopt in the Asian market. Hence Unilever has found that in order to sell more in sub-Saharan Africa, it must reduce the size of the package. The price must be reduced but the unit weight is cut proportionally. What customers in these markets spend on household goods has to remain in proportion to what they spend on other items, such as clothing, accommodation and food. A packet of soap powder costing disproportionately more than, say a loaf of bread, will appear too expensive; but if you reduce the price of that packet – albeit drastically reducing its contents in order to achieve that – you will make a sale even though the consumer is not paying less for the product. An interesting extension of this is that this same approach – smaller packages, lower prices – is now very effective in Greece, Spain and Portugal.

So what is the critical lesson for FMCGs? We believe the key is to evolve into FICGs – fast *innovating* consumer goods companies. Fast innovation entails leaving space for the consumer – halting the development and sales of finished, or finite, propositions and instead producing offerings that engage consumers and invite them to put the parts together on an individualised basis.

> 'The critical lesson for FMCGs is to evolve into FICGs – fast innovating consumer goods companies ... and to do that, they need to adopt a "Lego model."'

Some companies have always relied upon their customers to 'complete' the product for themselves. A perfect example is Lego, the Danish manufacture of building bricks for children. Originally, that's all Lego was: a range of interlocking plastic bricks that could be used to build model houses, towers, bridges and so on. Each brick was in itself utterly useless – the end user was the essential key to realising the product's value. This works extremely well because the value of the product is in its ability to stimulate the customer's imagination; it is an extremely creative product. But the thing the customer creates with the product is only temporary and is ultimately dismantled and put back in the box. The key to growing such a product is to add features that encourage and enable the user to explore new possibilities and develop their creativity.

During the 1980s, Lego started to introduce themes into its product, often linked to other products hitherto unconnected with it. Hence the success of the Star Wars range, the Harry Potter range and so on. This cleverly drew on the success of other brands, strengthening the Lego brand while at the same time expanding it. Other smart developments have included the release of Lego video games and even a range of children's clothes. After unsuccessful ventures into brand-linked, Disney-style amusement parks and hotels, and back-tracking on a decision to offshore all production to China, the company achieved all-time best results by returning to basics, concentrating on the essential building blocks and adding innovative features – small computers, engines and so on. Its latest innovation, announced in April 2013, is the first 'Lego school' in rural Jutland, which will deliver enquiry-based education from kindergarten through to the international baccalaureate. Lego has found a way to embody the values of its core product in a very different kind of deliverable:

'Allowing time for creativity, play and getting into a state of flow is at the centre of Lego's philosophy and we'll be experimenting with this and other ideas in the timetabling,' reported the school's new head teacher.[6]

The Lego story demonstrates that while diversification adds more to a company's portfolio it is acquisitive rather than innovative, whereas if a company concentrates on the core and thinks about renewal and add-ons, it is concentrating on consumers and innovating for them.

Recognising the decisive power of your customers – by which we mean not just their freedom to buy someone else's product, but also their power to dictate how your product should evolve – is essential. This has led to a strange and complex mixture of across-the-board standardisation and down-to-the-last-detail customisation. Several companies have developed ways of allowing the customer to create their own product, putting something together that they can feel is their own. So, for example, IKEA produces a multitude of household products and furniture, each one mass produced and identical to the next; and yet customers are encouraged to mix-and-match in a way that is very personal and creative. Another Scandinavian company, H&M, does the same with apparel.

Our 'Lego model' therefore proposes a route to regaining revenue and margin growth by incorporating features and elements that can generate excitement and innovation for the consumer. This adds value and relevance to the brand so that it does not rely on just one key product benefit, which is the raison d'être of all major marketing initiatives under the old school. Crucially, what the Lego model does is provide multiple ways of interacting with the consumer as they adopt and adapt the brand to their own requirements. Two brands that demonstrate a multiple touch-point approach are Jack Wills and Migros.

Launched in 1999, at around the time when British Prime Minister Tony Blair declared that he wanted 50 per cent of school leavers to continue into higher education, English clothing brand Jack Wills adopted a very traditional 'vintage' style and marketed itself as 'University Outfitters'. Sports sponsorship, exclusive ticket offers, music and brand ambassadors, or 'seasonnaires', who promote the brand at music festivals, holiday resorts and sporting events all provide different points of contact with the target customer group.

---

6   Russell, H. (2013) 'Lego school promises the building blocks to successful learning', *The Guardian*, 22 April.

The brand's image is of the archetypal middle- or upper-class, public-school Oxbridge student of the pre-War years, complete with tweeds and brogues. Its tag-line, usually found on all its products, is 'Fabulously British'. The clothes are expensive and the brand portrays itself as the antithesis of the working-class, football-themed ethos of other sports brands.

Thanks to Tony Blair's attempt to loosen the middle-class stranglehold on university education, more and more school leavers who might otherwise have chosen vocational courses or gone straight out to work now study for a degree. Jack Wills has tapped into this growing market and neatly undermined Blair by purveying an upper-class, retro image of varsity life as a step up the social ladder for fashion-conscious students. In so doing, it has prospered from the very bourgeois exclusivity that Blair (himself an Oxford graduate) hoped he'd killed.

The Jack Wills image is about a lot more than just the clothes. Customers can apply to receive its catalogues (styled as college prospectuses and called the 'Spring Term Handbook', the 'Autumn Term Handbook' and so on). The brand sponsors several sporting events, including the annual Oxford versus Cambridge university rugby match (the Varsity Match) at Twickenham. Soccer – an essentially working-class sport – is studiously ignored in favour of those that would be considered exclusive or upper-class: rowing, polo, skiing and rugby.

Careful to keep its customers engaged on all fronts, Jack Wills even has its own 'indie' music label featuring 'JW Unsigned' bands. No pre-war Oxbridge undergraduate would have understood that – but no matter, because customers can also buy tickets to watch Britain's top public schools, Eton and Harrow, battle it out on the polo field. They can also invest in skiing holidays where 'JW Ambassadors' make sure they will mix with the 'best' people. That all participants will inevitably all be decked out in Jack Wills apparel is probably a given.

Migros is the Swiss market leader in retailing, a unique organisation that is as close as a major corporation can come to being a non-profit organisation. Migros does not stock branded products; 99 per cent of its lines are its own. But Migros is much more than products and retailing. It has language schools that it finances from profit subsidy. It has banks. It has golf courses, including a top-notch 18-hole golf course between Lausanne and Geneva. It takes a lot of its profits and reinvests them in programmes for consumer education and consumer welfare. So Migros meets it customers on dozens of 'touch-points' every day – the Migros supermarket, the Migros credit card, the Migros loyalty card, the Migros golf course and so on. A Swiss citizen can run his or her life through Migros. But one major reason why Migros is thriving in the economic downturn is that it has recognised the breakdown in the norms of consumer behaviour. For example, the fastest growing part of Migros is its small neighbourhood Migrolino grocery stores, which are integrated into filling stations. Whenever customers fill up their car, they go into the store and they generally buy something. Even though the lines held in the smaller Migrolino stores are priced higher than in the big supermarkets, customers perceive the speed and convenience, together with the budget-price fuel, as valid trade-offs against the higher price of the perishables. Again, in its Migros Denner stores, where prices are slashed to the bone in a classic no-nonsense FMCG style, customers can buy expensive wines and cigars in the same environment as they buy their toilet paper and shampoo – big open cases, no frills, minimal display. Customers roll up in their BMWs to buy the cheapest toilet paper they can find and come away with a bottle of wine that costs 300 Swiss francs.

'At the back of every consumer's mind is a doubt that they are getting a fair deal.'

If this sounds counterintuitive it probably is; but Migros has identified two key facts that have changed the retail landscape. First, it acknowledges that the modern consumer can no longer be boxed or profiled in the time-honoured way in terms of where and how they shop, what products they buy and what their weekly spend is. Second, it recognises that at the back of every consumer's mind is a doubt that they are getting a fair deal, the misgiving that somehow, in some way, they are being done. The customer who spends as little as possible on toilet paper and washing powder will leave with a fistful of expensive cigars and feel good because he's sure he's got value for money. The head of Migrolino, Markus Laenzlinger, expressed it perfectly when he said that today companies 'don't compete on price; they compete on the fair deal'.

Chapter 2

The Rise of the Post-millennium Consumer

As the calendar clicked over at midnight on 31 December 1998, people around the world started to wonder what the last 12 months of the twentieth century would bring. This was the end of an era, the second millennium, the modern age. It was the sort of event that can be guaranteed to provoke introspection and encourage deep philosophical thoughts – especially after a few celebratory New Year's Eve drinks.

What did it mean to be on the cusp of a new era in human history and what would the next 100 years – never mind the next 1,000 – bring? The century that was drawing to a close was the most eventful in human history: it was the century that saw the dawn of powered flight and, less than a lifetime later, humans walking

> 'In the twentieth century the electron came to dominate our control and management of information, culminating in the creation, during the final decade, of the internet and the World Wide Web.'

on the face of the Moon. It was the century that twice witnessed the new horror of global mechanised warfare, and in which mankind harnessed – and unleashed – the awesome power of atomic energy. And it was the century in which a subatomic particle, the electron, came to dominate our control and management of information, culminating in the creation, during the final decade, of the internet and the World Wide Web.

It was only really during those final 12 months that the general population began to worry seriously about a curious flaw in mankind's computer technology, something that only computer experts had considered worth panicking about until then. Doom-mongering futurologists foresaw devastating repercussions from what became known as the Millennium or the Y2K Bug. The global consequences were believed to be potentially terminal. Planes, lifts and computer systems would be crashing worldwide and wholesale disaster would ensue. The canny among them saw business opportunities in the predicted disaster scenarios as major businesses, institutions and governments rang up hundreds of billions of dollars hedging against the environmental, health and financial implications of global IT dysfunction.

The problem that gave rise to the Millennium Bug was the simple and apparently harmless practice of recording year dates in double digits instead of four – such as '58 instead of 1958. For most of the century, this was standard shorthand and was readily adopted by the computer industry as it emerged in the latter half of the century. Of course the practice of using two-digit dates for convenience predates computers, but it was never a problem until stored dates were used in calculations. Computer systems that used the two-digit format were unable to distinguish between the years 2000 and 1900 and computer engineers quickly realised that this simple glitch could spell disaster. Date comparisons would deliver incorrect results and some computer systems could suffer complete failure. One of the greatest fears was that embedded systems, such as those used to control utilities, nuclear plants, air traffic control – and indeed the aircraft themselves – would fail. The lights would go off; nuclear reactors would go critical; communications would collapse. There would be global catastrophe.

As 1999 progressed, fear over the effects of the Millennium Bug spread. Stories in the press tended to play on the worst-case consequences and resisted any attempts to reassure the public. This was too good a story to play down and having whipped up a frenzy of concern, most newspapers were reluctant to countenance any evidence that the problem had been overblown.

The Millennium Bug phenomenon was real enough, however, and governments and businesses around the world started preparing for the worst. In September 1999 a 'last chance' guide for businesses still to tackle the Millennium Bug was launched by a special UK Government task force, Action 2000, set up to tackle the problem. Action 2000 estimated that over a quarter of a million of Britain's 1.3 million small-to-medium sized firms were still not ready, despite repeated warnings. The UK Environment Agency warned that the bug could cause widespread pollution because industry was doing too little to prepare for it.

Elsewhere, the World Health Organization (WHO) announced that it was worried about the 'unacceptably high' risk of a nuclear reactor accident within the next few years. The WHO's British physicist Dr Keith Baverstock told the

BBC that '31 December 1999 is one occasion when we ought to be even more vigilant than we normally are. The Millennium Bug is a real problem. We shall take it very seriously indeed.'[1]

As the deadline approached, emergency services around the world were put on full alert; in the UK, almost all police leave was cancelled over the New Year holiday and the government drew up plans to bring in the army should there be a complete collapse in essential services. Meanwhile the government monitoring centre prepared for initial reports coming in from Fiji and New Zealand shortly after noon on 31 December British time. John Battle, the Foreign Office minister, said he hoped the control centre would have 'a very boring time indeed'.

And so it did. With a very few exceptions, the Millennium Bug proved remarkably benign: one Japanese cell phone network found that some models of telephone were deleting new messages received, rather than old messages, as the memory filled up; several websites around the world gave the date as 1 January 19100; and 150 slot machines at racetracks in Delaware stopped working.

When the new millennium dawned without serious incident, the world breathed a huge sigh of relief and carried on with the routine business of getting and spending. Nothing seemed to have changed; in fact the Millennium Bug scare proved to be a complete anti-climax. The rapid development of mobile communications and computer technology that had characterised the last two decades of the twentieth century continued apace – indeed if anything it accelerated with an explosion in the use of mobile communications such as MSN text-messaging and wireless broadband internet.

However, although Armageddon did not descend on 1 January 2000, the rapid development of communications technology was changing the world in a way most businesses did not understand. There was indeed a significant threat facing commerce and industry but it wasn't one that anybody had anticipated. The Millennium Bug proved to be a chimera, an imagined threat and something that most terrified those with the least understanding. In the event, the predicted catastrophes did not happen – but something far

'There was indeed a significant threat facing commerce and industry but it wasn't one that anybody had anticipated. A new consumer emerged.'

---

1   BBC News, 27 November 1998, www.news.bbc.co.uk.

more subtle did: a new consumer emerged, surfing the e-waves and prepared to seize all the opportunities and possibilities they presented. And this new technology, unlike earlier technological advances (radio, television, air travel) had a more profound and irreversible qualitative impact. It created new attitudes, preferences and needs that translate into different choices.

Technological innovation in the first decade of the twenty-first century was characterised by the unprecedented empowerment of the consumer. If online shopping gave people almost unlimited choice, social networking gave them a voice. Traditional branding and the tendency to spoon-feed consumers with a mixture of seductive and dictatorial marketing fare worked well for the big brands throughout most of the twentieth century. But the arrival of blogging, interactive online news and social networks like Facebook and Twitter changed the marketing environment radically in the space of just a few years.

Since the dawn of the new millennium a new breed of consumer has emerged, a generation of mainly young, well-informed people whose chosen medium for news and entertainment is not the newspaper or the radio, nor even the television, but their portable device – their smart phone or tablet computer. These consumers consume brands, but they don't buy into traditional brand marketing the way previous generations did. They are more sceptical, less easy to seduce and more discerning, not only because they are better informed, but also because they are themselves more influential. In the interactive age, they have a voice.

This was nowhere more eloquently demonstrated than in the reaction to a song, written and performed by Canadian musician Dave Carroll and posted on the video sharing website YouTube in 2009. Carroll wrote the song, 'United Breaks Guitars', in frustration at the poor customer service he received from United Airlines, which he blamed for damaging his $3,500 Taylor guitar during a flight from Halifax, Nova Scotia, to Omaha, Nebraska. His song, written, recorded and posted on YouTube after nine months of fruitless negotiation with the airline, describes how Carroll and his fellow passengers watched in horror as baggage handlers threw Carroll's guitar onto the tarmac during a flight transfer at Chicago O'Hare. It included the memorable line, repeated at the end of each verse: 'I should have flown with someone else or gone by car, because United breaks guitars.'

The catchy song and its humorous video appeared on YouTube in early June 2009 and received 150,000 hits in the first day. The next day, United Airlines contacted Carroll offering compensation, but it was too late: within four days, United Airlines's stock price had fallen 10 per cent, wiping $180 million off the company's stock market value. By mid-August the video had gone viral. Three years later, the video was still going strong, having chalked up more than 12,500,000 hits.

United Airlines was, perhaps, unlucky but its experience at the hands of Dave Carroll demonstrates the power consumers now wield through the media of the internet and social networks. Other large and well-established brands have also suffered as a result of underestimating, or simply failing to understand, this new phenomenon.

Corporations such as United Airlines were slow to realise that the internet was altering their relationships with their customers. They saw it simply as a neat way of streamlining the existing process

> 'Consumers now wield a huge amount of power through the media of the internet and social networks.'

of sale and purchase, which it certainly was. Once the necessary security encryption methods had been perfected, so-called e-commerce began to take off and people were soon comfortable with online shopping – not only ordering online, but paying electronically too. Sites like eBay and Amazon were soon flourishing but with them came a new feature: the customer-feedback forum whereby purchasers could rate the product and the service provided by the retailer. This gave consumers far more power than they had previously enjoyed. Whereas a customer dissatisfied with the service provided by a vendor might previously have complained in writing (the exchange remaining strictly private between the two parties) they could now broadcast their dissatisfaction to the world.

The dawn of the new millennium did not itself bring about a seismic shift in the relationship between supplier and consumer; the two simply coincided. But while the world whipped itself into a frenzy of concern over the grossly overhyped threat of the Millennium Bug, many large and successful businesses failed to see the real danger being unleashed by the new technological age. The mobile phone had a central role in all this. Even 10 or 15 years before the end of the twentieth century the mobile phone had already become a symbol of success and sophistication. The huge, clunky Motorolas and Ericssons of the mid to late 1980s look ridiculous to today's users, but at the time they spoke of power and status. Their real power, however, only started to become apparent once they had reduced considerably in size and cost and could be afforded by ordinary people and not just yuppie wheeler-dealers.

The world of brand marketing really started to change when mobile phones became internet-enabled in the early years of this century. Anybody could now carry in their pocket the ability to broadcast their opinions to the world and convey information, both valuable and frivolous, via networking websites like Twitter and Facebook. Not surprisingly, the new technology industries that enabled this capability were the first to exploit it for marketing purposes. Apple, which has always packaged its products as seductively as possible (so successfully that the Apple brand is enduringly cool while main rival Microsoft is correspondingly geeky and gauche) found that by remaining aloof from traditional marketing wisdom – for example, by eschewing accepted market research methods and relying instead on its own instinctive feel for what its customers wanted – it could stimulate demand within its target markets.

However, although a cool brand, Apple also has its geeky following. The internet is awash with blogs, online magazines, forums and columnists who not only review new products but are sufficiently informed to predict trends and influence buyers. Apple knows better than most how to exploit these bloggers and reviewers. It uses this intelligence to keep one step ahead of the customer, making sure that no sooner is one product launched than its successor is stepping into the wings and ready to make its own entrance. The development of the iPad is typical: the original model attracted a storm of publicity and created such an appetite for innovation that Apple knew that customers would rush to buy the next-generation model the minute it was launched. Apple doesn't wait for its products to become obsolete or outdated: the original iPad is as capable and impressive now as it was at its launch in late 2010. Apple found that launching a new version doesn't affect demand for the original, which will still sell extremely well at a slightly lower price than the latest model.

Apple ensures that demand for its products remains continually high by 'teasing' the market. A favourite ploy, developed by Apple boss Steve Jobs, is to hold a press conference announcing the imminent launch of a new product, outlining the key features and proposed innovations. This stimulates widespread media commentary with everybody from the mainstream media to teenage bloggers joining in debate over the pros and cons of Apple's proposed innovations. The Apple marketing team simply sits back and follows the discussion, taking note of which features are welcomed and which are derided, and briefing the R&D department accordingly. When the product is finally launched (a vigorously hyped event which itself invariably receives extensive media coverage) it ticks all the right boxes on the wish lists of the world's technology cognoscenti.

Companies like Apple have thrived in the early years of the new millennium. So have many smaller companies that have either sprung out of the internet age or shown enough agility and insight to embrace the new world order. But many established brands have struggled to make that transition. In many cases, these companies have built brands into household names over several decades and sustained them using established marketing methods that are no longer as effective as they were. Glib advertising slogans that fail to engage with customers are simply disregarded today; branding must be interactive and personal – a phenomenon exemplified by the now common ploy of explicitly implying the consumer's ownership: 'Your M&S' and 'My BT', for example.

However, there is no law that says that big, long-established multinationals cannot use the marketing methods employed by young, fast-growing companies like Apple. The only factor that sets them apart is attitude of mind. Companies that can see ahead and are prepared to adapt will prevail. Those that cling to the belief that what made their brand successful in the last century must be preserved at all costs are doomed to failure.

Traditional FMCG companies have failed to recognise the new breed of consumer and that is a serious problem for them. Most of the classic FMCG markets in the developed world are either saturated or are evolving faster than the companies themselves can accommodate. As they struggle to compete with generic products and other value-for-money providers supplying good-enough products at much lower prices, the old-school FMCGs find themselves in a price trap with little money in the budget for R&D, much of which is now outsourced, and unable to innovate. It is a downward spiral and many of these old companies are relying increasingly on emerging markets in the developing world. The trouble is, given the pace of global change, they will soon have the same problem across these markets too.

> *'Traditional FMCG companies have failed to recognise the new breed of consumer and that is a serious problem for them.'*

> *'Change is scary for big, old organisations but not changing is even scarier for smaller, newer organisations.'*

The only breakthrough seems to have come from companies that we would not previously have categorised as FMCGs – computers, internet, mobile phones, social networking and, surprisingly, luxury brand staples. Change is scary for big, old organisations but not changing is even scarier for smaller, newer organisations.

It would be wrong to conclude that FMCGs and their marketing specialists had failed to foresee a revolution in communication technology. In fact they had anticipated it by at least ten years, having observed the global penetration of the internet and the explosion in mobile telephony. Their mistake was to assume that it was just the medium of communication that was changing and that the message would stay the same. They stuck resolutely to their old tried-and-tested principles of advertising and marketing (the big picture, one-sentence tag lines, mnemonic slogans, the sanctity of the single consumer end benefit leading to the unique selling point) and consequently they all use social networks as a medium to communicate old strategies instead of changing the way they approach their customers.

So in what way are modern consumers so different? Colin Campbell, Professor of Sociology at the University of York, explains that psychologically and emotionally, consumer behaviour is becoming less needs-based: 'Modern consumerism is by its very nature predominately concerned with the gratification of wants rather than the meeting of needs. The significance of this development being that, while needs can be, and indeed generally are, objectively established, wants can only be identified subjectively. That is to say, others can always tell you what it is that you need ... But no one but you is in a position to decide what it is that you want. When it comes to wanting only the "wanter" can claim to be an "expert".'[2] Modern consumerism, according to Campbell, is 'fiercely individualistic' and consumers today build their identity on the basis of their reactions to available products. As a result of this, and with their handheld devices acting as information portals to a whole new world of spending opportunities, modern consumers shop in a completely different way from previous generations. Smart phones and tablets have swept away the centuries-old retail traditions of the shop window and customer service and have had an impact out of all proportion to their size.

'Smart phones and tablets have swept away the centuries-old retail traditions of the shop window and customer service.'

Let's consider how the modern consumer shops today – and let's start by jettisoning the idea of shopping as an expedition requiring weather-appropriate outerwear and route planning, because the modern consumer may never leave the house. Here's how we observed one 16-year-old girl, raised in Brighton and visiting New York for the first time, shopping for clothes.

---

2   Campbell, C. (2004) 'I Shop therefore I Know that I Am', in Ekström, K.M. and Brembeck, H. (eds), *Elusive Consumption*, Berg, New York.

First, there was the pre-shopping to be done. She started on her computer in her hotel room, deciding which item, which brand, which shop, consulting various blogs and checking what her friends were saying. She narrowed her search down to four items in three shops, then took her smart phone and went to Google Earth, which told her exactly where to find the stores she wanted in the city. Only then did she leave the hotel room. In the store she contacted her three best friends: one was in Japan on holiday, another on an internship in Hamburg and the third at home in the UK. She photographed the dress, told them the store only had it in red and sent them the picture. The three friends got the picture of the item in the store in New York simultaneously and texted her with their opinions.

This 16-year-old girl was thinking about buying a dress; but in a very short time she will be shopping the same way for financial services, a washing machine, a car, maybe even an apartment. She is the future of the modern consumer and completely different from the consumer we are used to. Companies need to be ready for her. Her decision-making process is not the one marketers have been targeting for the past 50 years – in which the television tells you what to buy before you venture out to find it yourself in the shop. Today's consumers want more than that from a marketer. Dealing with the new consumer is not just a question of understanding behaviour, or coming to grips with the new technology. It achieves nothing to bombard multi-tasking, multi-dimensional consumers with repetitive single-minded messages.

Retailers need to know how to deal with a consumer who comes in already knowing what is on the shelf and whose purchasing decision is contingent on something completely out of the manufacturer's or retailer's control – such as what her friend in Japan is going to say about the dress in the photo she's just mailed to her. The first thing is to drop the idea that the retailer is selling: the transactional element of the retail experience has taken a back seat and now it's about service and identification with the consumer: 'I am your friend, I understand you, I'm just like you and I'm here to help.' Retailers have not only to accommodate the consumer who wants to photograph or handle the stock but actively encourage them to do so.

As in so many other areas, Apple has led the field in redefining the retail experience. In its stores customers are encouraged to come in and play – the polar opposite of the stores many of us will remember from our childhood where we were firmly told 'look, don't touch'. Its emotional design language also creates appeal that cuts across old perceptions and all kinds of cultural boundaries. The old traditional roles of shopper and sales assistant are redefined, or rather they've had their definitions blurred to the point where distinguishing one from the other would challenge any casual observer unfamiliar with Apple's philosophy. Customers are encouraged to handle the goods without a pushy shop assistant breathing down their neck. They can simply wander in from the street and play with the products while Apple staff circulate informally, engaging customers in the sort of conversation they might expect to have with friends at home or at work. They might even be on first name terms within a couple of minutes. There's no room in these stores for the scary salesperson who patronises, hassles or embarrasses customers into a sale. And Apple staff live the brand. Every person in the store is linked by an iPad or iPhone and cross-communicates. The transactional element is also informalised. There is no cash desk; the assistant takes a card payment with a handheld reader and the customer picks up the goods from a collection point in store.

> *'Customers today expect to have more say in the finished product they buy and to be part of the process.'*

The consumer empowerment that accompanies increased knowledge is another significant factor in the changing retail experience. Customers today expect to have more say in the finished product they buy and to be part of the process. Anybody who has bought a new car recently will be aware of the opportunity to exercise their creativity, compare the distinguishing features of different brands and specifications, specify colour and finishing options, and end up with a tailored product at a bespoke price. The consumers are very happy because they feel they have used their own intelligence and creativity in making the product up, and their informed, fact-based approach has been duly acknowledged by the retailer.

Ingvar Kamprad, the founder of international home products company IKEA, lives by this principle. He maintains that the whole point of its business model is that it makes consumers feel happy in much the same way: the store releases their creativity.[3] This might seem paradoxical when every store worldwide stocks the same lines and the company promotes its products across all cultural and continental divides (with the occasional well-publicised exception) through the same catalogue. Yet creativity is the keynote of the company's success just as much as affordability. People can browse the store or catalogue and create their own living spaces, furnishings, colour themes and so on; they can construct an entire context for themselves and it makes them feel great.

---

3   Torekull, B. (2009) *Slik gjorde jeg det! Eventyret Ingvar Kamprad – mannen som pakket verden flat*, Publicom; Kamprad, I. (1976) *The Testament of a Furniture Dealer*, Inter IKEA Systems, Delft; Tonkall, B. (2006) *Historien om IKEA*, Walström and Widstrand, Stockholm; Tarnovskaya, V.V. and de Chernatory, L. (2011) 'Internalizing a brand across cultures: the case of IKEA', *International Journal of Retail and Distribution Management*, 39 (8), pp. 598–618.

This touches on a point that we will return to in this book many times: control of supply. The old model was that a company produced the goods then handed them over to a distribution and retail chain that did the rest. But this model is surely redundant when today's consumers are so far ahead of the curve that they are interacting with the manufacturer almost on a one-to-one basis via Facebook, Twitter or other electronic media.

Modern consumers are completely at ease with communications technology. They have faith in the internet – they trust it more than they would trust a salesperson: it's difficult to hide negative facts when bloggers, commentators and social networking sites distribute knowledge and informed opinion in an environment which is essentially one of transparency. Some brands seek to exploit this fact by conducting 'advocacy' campaigns on the internet – effectively harnessing the power of the personal recommendation. 'A personal recommendation is more powerful than an advert. Who takes the advice of advertising over their friends? No one,' declares teenage entrepreneur and party promoter Callum Negus-Fancey. 'If a person I know and trust makes a recommendation to me, I listen. That is the crux of brand advocacy, the acknowledgment that personal recommendations are powerful and that they are influencing consumer purchases every day.'[4] The flipside of this, of course, is obvious: 'Brands that fail to put their house in order before attempting an advocacy programme face the very real threat of "badvocates". Badvocates have the potential to damage a brand's reputation and sales figures as much as advocates can enhance them.'[5] Modern consumers are becoming activists: they are used to the speed and facility of instant communication; they want responses to their feedback right now. And the message for the marketing industry is: 'If you lie, you die.'

So instead of pumping out a consistent, unvarying corporate message to all potential consumers via advertising and traditional marketing avenues, corporations now need to concentrate on building networks that allow them to befriend their customers. They need to establish interactive relationships with them in order to build trust and loyalty. These networks are the route to new customers who are brought on board by word of mouth, by personal recommendation and the desire to become part

> 'Corporations now need to concentrate on building networks that allow them to befriend their customers.'

---

4   Negus-Fancey, C. (2011) 'There's no such thing as an original good idea', posted on the *Huffington Post*, 6 October.
5   Negus-Fancey, C. (2011) '"Badvocates" and advocacy marketing', posted on the *Huffington Post*, 7 November.

of an ongoing dialogue with other like-minded people via an online social network. It is of course the smaller, younger, more nimble companies that do this best. These companies, with their flat management structures and lean workforces can make rapid changes to the way they conduct business. Most have had to grow quickly and that is not easy if you have constantly to recruit and train people. It is much quicker to buy in new skills from other specialists, and so these companies have become adept at outsourcing.

Every company outsources to some degree; it is traditionally seen as a handy way of reducing fixed overheads and introducing flexibility into an organisation. But you have to know what to outsource. If you simply outsource the costliest functions you might find yourself giving away your competitive edge and losing control of your key capability. It is essential to identify what it is that you do better than anyone else and keep it in-house. For example, route to market can give you competitive edge. It's easy to outsource but difficult to use as an added-value tool – so if route to market is your key advantage, keep control of it. This also applies to certain routine functions that have a direct impact on your key capabilities. The pinnacle of absurdity of outsourcing is human resources. What happens when companies get other people to run their own human resources (HR)? They end up hiring people with identical profiles and CVs because the pre-selection is done mechanically and too much emphasis is placed on academic achievement. Beyond administration, HR has two fundamental roles. The first is attracting and developing future leaders, which is the key to sustaining greatness. The second is maintaining the integral culture of the company, which is the main reason why people stay with and do not just work for their pay. This can only be done in-house and is a vital element of what sets a company apart. In-house HR knows what qualities the company needs and can look beyond exam performance when scouting for young talent; this is particularly relevant to the latest generation of fast-growing technology start-ups, a significant proportion of which seem to be founded by young university drop-outs for whom the conventional selection criteria matter little. Outsourcing HR helps with efficiency – but not with effectiveness.

Despite the self-evident wisdom of holding on to your core strengths, more and more central functions in big companies are being outsourced and not just for cost-cutting reasons. Older companies that do not consider the fast-evolving world of mobile communication and social networking to be a core discipline are happy to outsource important functions such as the company website – essentially the company's shop window and the first point of contact for a great many customers. It is vitally important that co-ordination of marketing and product innovation are both kept in-house and, in today's environment, that requires somebody at the top of the organisation to oversee the new online presence and co-ordinate the networking capability – a new management function for most companies.

Perhaps the most important characteristic of this new breed of networked organisations is responsiveness and the ability to make more or less continuous innovations in line with customer expectations. To do this effectively, a networked company must have excellent internal communications as well as communicating well with its customers. Marketing and R&D have always had to work together, the one identifying what the market wants, the other finding ways of providing it. But to operate successfully as a networked organisation, the business has to break down internal divisions, get rid of the silo mentality and work as a genuinely integrated team. If you can dissolve these internal barriers you have a better chance of really understanding the key consumer within your market sector. You also reduce the risk of 'committee overload' arising from an attempt to address every category of customer. With an integrated team culture in place of the traditional departmental one, there is less scope for confrontation and less energy is wasted in quarrelling about strategy and the division of roles.

Innovation, marketing and communication all need to work together in the line, not in the R&D lab, or in the central marketing or in communications departments. What drives innovation today is not whatever is going on in the lab; it's the people who are close to the relevant customers.

This affects the types of innovation we see as well. First, they tend to be small and incremental. Second, to keep their existing consumers on board, instead of rolling out brand new

> 'To operate successfully as a networked organisation, the business has to break down internal divisions, get rid of the silo mentality and work as a genuinely integrated team.'

products, companies focus on making good products even better. Third, they are communicable – they make sense to the consumer. For example, modern consumers respond enthusiastically to an innovation that means their mobile phone will connect twice as fast or the battery lasts twice as long. It's not a new type of mobile phone but it's a better phone.

Organisations have to be able to match the speed, agility, rapid adaptation and response rates of their customers. This implies strong networking between different executive levels, companies and their customers, as well as leading professional associations, and so on. But why should other firms allow their key associates to work with emerging networked entities? The fact is that a networked context may tempt an executive to try out new things in a safe space, where the risk of failure may not have the same implications it does 'at home', where rewards are linked to performance appraisal and reviews. Imported innovation may mean faster speed to market as well, bypassing the need for endless internal debates.

> 'Today's consumers see little value in promises of large, earth-shattering discoveries that won't see the light of day until far into the future. But incremental improvements that they can understand do have value.'

The traditional image of innovation is that it is something that happens in large, expensive, centralised R&D departments, where people work on important projects with far-reaching potential to change the future. Regrettably, this type of R&D often leads to little or nothing or the results are delivered too late. Today's consumers want evidence of progress now. They see little value in promises of large, earth-shattering discoveries that won't see the light of day until far into the future. But incremental improvements that they can understand do have value. So there is a lot to be said for improving or enhancing traditional products that are already good enough and deliver generic benefits. Innovation should not, therefore, be driven by what the engineers find exciting in the R&D lab so much as by what the marketing and communications people are picking up from the consumers with whom they are networked. Hence the small, incremental 'breakthroughs' that steadily bring about improvements in line with customer expectations. That is not to say that you cannot surprise your customers – indeed you should – but to do so you must be able to predict the sort of improvements that they will value. Don't invent a radically new product if there's no customer expectation to justify the innovation – but do introduce improvements to a successful existing product if there are signs that the customer is ready to accept them.

A very good example of how this is done is the following story of how a new market was developed for one very basic, everyday product – and how the Portuguese company Renova made toilet paper the 'must-have' must have.

The toilet paper business is not a glamorous career option, which maybe explains why neither of Paulo Pereira da Silva's parents had chosen to join the family firm founded by Paulo's grandfather in the 1930s. However, Paulo felt differently. In 1984, having graduated in Physical Engineering from Ecole Polytechnique Fédérale de Lausanne in Switzerland, he returned to his native Portugal and joined the family business, paper company Renova, as a production manager. In the early 1960s, Renova had shifted away from its original market for office paper to concentrate on disposable tissues and hygiene products. By the time Paulo joined, 50 per cent of the company's business was in toilet paper and Renova was market leader in this sector, its Super brand being the country's oldest and best-selling brand with 25 per cent market share. On the other hand, the toilet paper market not only lacked glamour but was also highly commoditised: there was little potential for growth. When Portugal joined the European Union (EU) in 1986, Renova took this opportunity to address the wider European market; but EU membership also meant that Renova faced growing competition on its home turf from the likes of global giants Procter & Gamble and Kimberley-Clark. The major retail chains such as Carrefour, Lidl and Tesco also brought competition with their own brands of toilet paper – and these retailers were also Renova's biggest clients.

With the largest share of Portugal's €135 million toilet paper market, Renova had a lot to lose but very limited opportunity for growth and development. Market saturation and a stable population meant that the Portuguese market for disposable paper products was growing at less than 1.5 per cent per annum. By 1995, Paulo da Silva had worked his way up the corporate ladder to the top rung: he was CEO. A strong believer in branding and product innovation, he was not satisfied simply to maintain Renova's position in the domestic marketplace. With competition on every side, he resolved to raise his game and grow the brand. To do that, though, Renova would have to look outside Portugal. In a European market worth about €20 billion the company commanded a share of less than 1 per cent, the bulk of sales being accounted for by the established international players. Profitability in this industry is generally low and is strongly influenced by energy prices. So how could Renova, with no clear cost advantage, no distinctive brand positioning and no unique product features, grow its business and expand into new markets?

Da Silva started by reorganising the company, taking out several layers of management to produce a lean, flat structure designed to encourage innovation and permit more creative risk-taking. Da Silva didn't see why, just because the company made toilet paper, Renova could not be innovative, dynamic and creative. He personally redesigned the Renova offices, getting rid of partitions to create an open-plan space. He even designed some of the new furniture himself. His most important decision, however, was to look beyond the business of making disposable paper products towards a more appealing and marketable role as a provider and guardian of personal health and well-being. Renova, after all, was about personal hygiene products that, although hitherto unfashionable, are fundamental to maintaining a happy, healthy lifestyle. Along with the new image, Renova needed to transform itself into a premium brand as only a premium toilet paper stood any chance of growth. To convey this new identity, da Silva engaged top advertising agencies and fashion photographers to produce stylish eye-catching advertisements that showed the core product – toilet paper – in a new and unconventional light. His promotional budget rose to €1.5 million a year.

Of course Renova also needed to develop its product range in order to justify its claim to be a premium brand. Innovation in the toilet tissue industry is rare, but not unknown. Market research (which found that a large number of users habitually wet paper before use) had already resulted in the development of moist wipes. Renova, in fact, was the first company to introduce moist toilet paper to the Iberian Peninsula, though the business benefits were modest since moist wipes represent less than one per cent of the Portuguese market. In 1998, Renova was also the first to introduce impregnated paper – treated with moisturising lotions and balms – to Spain and Portugal. This product, Renova Fraîcheur, was also instrumental in getting Renova a foothold in the French market. While novelty toilet paper (with such whimsical features as Christmas designs or the faces of unpopular public figures) has always been produced, it has never amounted to a significant market sector. Pastel coloured papers, however, were very popular in the 1970s and 1980s before falling out of fashion again during the 1990s.

One thing nobody had done before, however, was produce black toilet paper. It was during a Las Vegas performance by avant-garde entertainment group Cirque du Soleil, as acrobats performed above the audience, suspended on black silk ribbons, that da Silva got his idea. Black is always fashionable, but it was unheard of in the disposable paper sector. Renova Black certainly created a lot of publicity for the company – for the first time, people were talking about toilet paper and buying it for the perceived cachet. Other strong colours – fuchsia, orange, royal blue – followed soon after, along with stylish and expensive packaging. The strategy has been so successful that Renova now produces toilet paper gift packs.

Renova experienced a rapid increase in brand awareness and market research showed that the brand was particularly well regarded by young, wealthy adults from the upper reaches of the social scale. Through targeted advertising and online PR, Renova stimulated interest in target export markets, creating a buzz even before the official launch of the product. In 2006 *The New York Times* carried a story focusing on the appearance of this exotic black toilet paper in a fashionable Manhattan nightclub.[6]

---

6   Green, P. (2006) 'This Season's Must-Have: The Little Black Roll', *New York Times*, 18 May.

Today, Renova is a highly value-added niche player that has successfully sidestepped the dominant multinational giants in a low-margin, commodity-driven market. Since 2006, while increasing its leading share of the domestic market, Renova has massively increased exports to the point where approximately 50 per cent of sales are now to overseas markets. Nobody else has yet succeeded in making toilet paper desirable, fashionable and artistic. And who would ever have thought you could give toilet paper as a gift?[7]

Innovations today happen at the interface between the consumer and the product or service provider. Da Silva could never have launched a black toilet paper had he not understood his customer

> 'Innovations today happen at the interface between the consumer and the product or service provider.'

base and calculated that this product enhancement would appeal. It is hard for classic, centralised R&D units to respond like this and so innovation must be seen as part of marketing. Instant feedback – so valuable and so accessible from the internet – leads to instant modifications of products and services. In the past, customers themselves have been the innovators, tinkering away at home to improve off-the-shelf products or modifying them to satisfy their own requirements.

Professor Eric von Hippel, an expert on user innovation, describes this as 'the dark matter of innovation – a new pattern for how innovations come about'.[8] In 2010, von Hippel and his colleagues completed the first-ever large-scale survey of user innovation for the British government, and found that 'the amount of money individual consumers spent making and improving products was more than twice as large as the amount spent by all British firms combined on product research and development over a three-year period'.[9]

A classic example of user innovation is the story of Walt Blackader, a US kayaker who 40 years ago changed the face of his sport. Kayaking is typical of the kind of activity where enthusiasts and amateur inventors abound. Hienerth et al. (2011) found that innovative users at the leading edge of the sport each spent an average of $707 and 27 days a year on creating and

7 Chandon, P., Bart, Y., Sweldens, S. and Seabra de Sousa, R. 'Renova Toilet Paper: Avant-garde Marketing in a Commoditized Category', INSEAD, Ref 510-077-1.
8 Cohen, P. (2011) 'Innovation far removed from the lab', *The New York Times*, 9 February.
9 Cohen, P. (2011) 'Innovation far removed from the lab', *The New York Times*, 9 February.

improving kayaking equipment.[10] Walt Blackader was one of these, a US kayaker who got a kick from the more dangerous methods of whitewater kayaking – entering waves sideways on, or even backwards. His exploits attracted other enthusiasts, or 'extreme paddlers', and before long they were adapting and making specialised fibreglass kayaks and safety equipment to help them in the water. Newcomers to the sport began commissioning boats from them and before long commercial manufacturers noticed the trend and started producing cheaper, if less adaptable, plastic versions. Meanwhile, user-innovators continued to fine-tune their fibreglass versions for competitive events until eventually both the enthusiasts and the manufacturers were developing rapidly in response to each other. Increasing numbers of people were drawn to what had become a new style of kayaking and by 2000, 30 years after Walt Blackader had challenged himself to ride a wave backwards, 'rodeo kayaking' had become an established sport and a definitive, standard rodeo kayak design had emerged.[11]

Crucially, to be sustainable the cost of R&D must be incurred where the pay-off is highest. Only incremental innovations that build on what already exists can ensure this. For all these reasons, centralised R&D units are on their way out and increasingly distributed R&D is on the way in. This is less a matter of overall cost savings than of ensuring that consumers are involved in incremental innovations – and it brings us back to the ultimate test: the consumer must understand the value of an innovation, and be willing to pay for it. A brand is one of the few asset classes that are still associated with scale – a global brand can be extremely powerful. It is of course expensive to build, and it takes time, so financial resources are critical. But of course this does not imply that only the old, large corporate models have the financial muscle for brand building; network-based companies can do the same by involving consumers. In fact, networks have built today's biggest global brands – household names that have been established in record time – Google, Amazon, Baidu, eBay and Yahoo, all founded between 1994 and 1999, are internet-only businesses. And Apple now vies with ExxonMobil for the title of the world's largest company, even temporarily pushing the oil giant into second place in 2012.[12] A brand that does not live up to consumers' expectations today can be quickly damaged.

---

10 Hienerth, C., Jensen, M.B. and von Hippel, E. (2011) 'Innovation as consumption: Analysis of consumers' innovation efficiency', MIT Sloan School of Management Working Paper.
11 Baldwin, C., Hienerth, C. and von Hippel, E. (2006) 'How user innovations become commercial products: A theoretical investigation and case study', Harvard Business School Working Paper 06 032.
12 Russollilo, S. (2013) 'Apple loses throne as world's biggest company', Wall Street Journal, 17 April.

Before the internet age, negative publicity could largely be brushed aside; people have short memories and one day's bad press used to be the next day's fish-and-chip wrapper. But the internet's memory is not only more enduring, it is also potentially infinite. Bad publicity and negative feedback, once online, can be dredged up any time; they never go away. Reputation management is now critical and companies must remain vigilant and swift to respond to what their customers are saying about them online – both positive and negative. Thus innovation is 'policed' by the consumer – and only legitimate innovations will survive.

What happens when a brand that embodies traditional values, such as quality, dependability and familiarity, decides to attract a new, young clientele? Burberry, the UK-based fashion brand, got it wrong first time round but, having learned its lesson, went on to demonstrate the power of tapping into today's networked consumer. Roughly ten years ago, Burberry embarked on a brand relaunch. Tapping into the excitement surrounding the dawn of the new millennium, the company turned to a new and much younger audience, launching a range of youth-oriented products bearing its distinctive Burberry check design. Soon the Burberry check was everywhere. Traditionally used mainly as a lining for the company's famous trenchcoats and other garments, the design became the focus of the new campaign and was used extensively throughout the product range. Handbags, umbrellas, shirts, trousers and even baby clothes all sported the Burberry check, but nothing proclaimed the brand's desperation to attract the youth market more loudly than the Burberry check baseball cap. The appearance of this accessory is seen by many as the point at which the campaign came off the rails.

> *'Innovation is "policed" by the consumer – and only legitimate innovations will survive.'*

Despite (or perhaps because of) the endorsement of top model Kate Moss, whose emerging reputation for louche behaviour and an unhealthy lifestyle struck a chord with the wrong social group, Burberry quickly became the designer of choice for young, white men and women from low-income social groups known disparagingly as 'chavs'. The brand relaunch had backfired disastrously. Instead of becoming the standard-bearer for young, chic, discerning purchasers, Burberry found itself the unofficial badge of a feral underclass. The label quickly back-pedalled, drastically reducing the visibility of its now overexposed check design to shake off the 'chav' image. In 2009, with clean-cut Harry Potter actress Emma Watson as the new face of Burberry, the brand focused once more on its core product, the quintessentially British trenchcoat. Having pulled back from the brink and now more aligned with its original target customers, Burberry seized upon the social networking phenomenon to raise its profile in this sector. Under the leadership of new CEO Angela Ahrendts, the company built up a strong following on Facebook (attracting 660,000 'friends' – more than any other luxury brand, according to Ahrendts). But then in late 2009 it went further and launched its own social networking site: artofthetrench.com. The site, which allows users to upload photographs of themselves wearing Burberry trenchcoats and share comments with other users, aims to build brand loyalty and attract new customers. It features real people wearing Burberry coats, has music tracks from new and upcoming British pop groups embedded in it and creates a buzz which, according to Ahrendts, 'invites them into the brand – especially the younger customer – more than the stores do'.

> *These [people] might not even be customers yet – or they might be a customer for a bottle of fragrance or for eyewear. But these are customers who need the brand experience, who need to feel the brand. That word-of-mouth spreads through their social networks and continues to be a positive conversation that is so powerful.*[13]

Although it retains its chain of stores, Burberry now relies more heavily on electronic social networks to spread the word and draw in new customers. Successful Facebook and Twitter campaigns can quickly attract tens of thousands of 'followers' and, with virtually no investment, can create the sort of exposure normally costing hundreds of thousands in television and print advertising. But Burberry's strategy is not just about numbers. Ahrendts even goes so far as to say that, for sheer brand experience, stores cannot compete with electronic social networks. 'You go into a store, you might not even notice the music playing,' she says, pointing out that at artofthetrench.com the music is an integral feature of the experience and creates an instant ambience. Added to this the inherent interactivity of social networking quickly draws visitors to the site into a dialogue with other users to create a sense of community that cannot be so easily conjured up simply by walking into a store. 'It's sometimes even more of a three-dimensional experience [online] because you have so many other things you can play with,' she says.

For example, an online video of famous fashion photographers shooting the latest Burberry ads provides a privileged glimpse into a glamorous world that cannot be provided in print or in stores. 'It's that kind of "behind-the-scenes" that the customer wants. That's the new form of entertainment and

---

13 Edgar, R. (2009) 'Burberry looks to win over friends online', *Financial Times*, 26 September.

that invites them into the brand,'[14] declares Ahrendts. The strategy seems to be working. In 2011 Burberry was one of the top ten companies showing the biggest growth in brand value, with 20 per cent growth increasing the value of sales to $3.7 billion and moving Burberry from 100th to 95th place in the Interbrand annual ranking.

Brand is particularly critical for luxury goods manufacturers but they have embraced web-based marketing and sales with enthusiasm[15] – surprising, considering their high level of vulnerability, including the risk of counterfeiting and the importance of 'exclusivity' for their image. So why are the internet and luxury goods companies increasingly friends? First of all, they can't afford not to be, given today's level of online shopping. Second, the internet offers a new slant on exclusivity: discreet and personal shopping from the privacy of your computer screen. Third, the internet enables luxury goods companies to retain high-end appeal and high prices. In principle, there is no discounting or sales but discretionary sites offer 'last season's' designs at lower prices.

> 'Luxury goods manufacturers have embraced web-based marketing and sales with enthusiasm.'

At first it seems thoroughly anomalous – making limited edition luxury items available through a public website and boutique shopping from your office desk. Yet Natalie Massenet makes it work at Net-a-Porter, a unique combination of glossy magazine and online retail outlet. Massenet did not choose the most auspicious time to launch her online luxury fashion business. It was 2000, businesses were bracing themselves for the impact of the Millennium Bug and the dot.com bubble was about to burst. At about the same time as Massenet launched Net-a-Porter, another online clothing retailer failed spectacularly: Boo.com went under having blown $135 million of venture capital in just two years. But Massenet was not deterred. She could see a gap in the market.

Massenet knew the fashion business well. The daughter of an American journalist and an English Chanel model, she had worked as a professional stylist and, before launching the new business, worked as a fashion writer for *Tatler* magazine. Her idea of online fashion retailing differed fundamentally from the existing model. Whereas other sites just posted pictures and descriptions

---

14 Edgar, R. (2009) 'Burberry looks to win over friends online', *Financial Times*, 26 September.
15 Clark, A. (2011) 'Rise of the Apple iPad puts Apple within touching distance of the biggest brands', *The Times*, October 5.

online with the sole aim of selling products, Massenet wanted her site to be part virtual shop, part fashion magazine. The products would all be there, but within the context of an editorial commentary that would include feature articles and picture stories looking at various aspects of the fashion industry. As a fashion writer, Massenet's ambition had been to become a magazine editor. But ten years after launching Net-a-Porter she told *The Observer*:

> *I hadn't walked away from being editor-in-chief of a magazine – I'd just created a magazine for the twenty-first century instead, a hybrid between a store and a magazine that was delivered digitally.*[16]

This way of shopping online was entirely new when Massenet launched Net-a-Porter into a sceptical market; even today many online retailers rely solely on the ease and convenience of internet shopping and make little effort to engage the purchaser. This can work well for traditional FMCGs such as groceries, books, household goods and so on. But shopping for luxury products, especially clothes, tends to be a more personal, even emotional, experience. The received wisdom ten years ago was that someone who was prepared to spend £500 on luxury fashion items during one visit (the average spend per visit at Net-a-Porter today) would need to see, feel and try on the clothes first. In the early days of Net-a-Porter, Massenet struggled to get top brands to do business with her. 'Every conversation ended with them saying "So where's your store?" she recalls. But Net-a-Porter's online store-cum-magazine did so much more than simply parade the products in front of the customer that, as one fashion commentator remarked, 'Customers don't just buy; they're told what to buy.' And by creating a convincing online brand presence, Massenet proved that people were more than willing to buy luxury clothes without first trying them on.

One of the paradoxes that major brands found difficult to reconcile was the fact that Net-a-Porter places a high value on customer care without ever having a physical relationship with its customers. The only face-to-face interaction between the customer and the retailer is when the courier delivers the order – long after the sale has been concluded and the goods paid for. But by creating a vibrant and constantly changing online presence, Net-a-Porter makes the shopping experience exciting and absorbing. Users can browse the site purely for entertainment, just as they would when picking up a fashion magazine during a coffee break. And Net-a-Porter's weekly online magazine is a genuine, well-written and professionally designed periodical. Customers report that the shopping experience at Net-a-Porter is not only easy, but also highly enjoyable.

---

16 Wiseman, E. (2010) 'One-click wonder: the rise of Net-a-Porter', *The Observer*, 11 July.

The trick, however, is that the experience takes place within the virtual 'shop' of the Net-a-Porter site and purchases can be easily made simply by clicking on the appropriate image within the magazine or elsewhere on the site.

The online environment is also a good place to persuade people to part with their money. Customers enter the site from the safe and familiar surroundings of their office desk or kitchen table and can shop in a relaxed mood where they are in control. There's no sales assistant to breathe down their neck. Visiting Net-a-Porter is more like window-shopping than real shopping and clicking to buy something feels less real than handing over your card to a sales assistant.

Lucy Yeomans, fashion editor at *Harper's Bazaar* and a former colleague of Massenet's at *Tatler*, told *The Observer* that she buys something from Net-a-Porter about once a fortnight, usually while on the move between appointments 'because time is so precious. And I hate changing rooms.' Another fashion professional, Siobhan Mallen, fashion editor with *Grazia* magazine, admits to visiting Net-a-Porter every day. She says the secret of the site is the 'edit': 'They have the best choice of the best labels in the world. The fact they deliver to your desk is an added bonus.'[17] This prompt delivery is indeed a vital element of the Net-a-Porter model, as is presentation of the goods. Clothes are delivered in distinctive, expensive-looking black boxes tied up with grosgrain ribbon. Inside, the clothes are carefully wrapped in crisp pink tissue paper. One of the secrets of Net-a-Porter's huge success is that every purchase comes dressed as a gift.

The formula has proved phenomenally successful. Net-a-Porter has been profitable from its inception and today is valued at more than £135 million. It never stands still and has recently launched The Outnet, a parallel site selling discounted stock from previous collections, and Mr Porter, a menswear equivalent to the original site. In September 2011 Net-a-Porter started experimenting with Aurasma, an 'augmented reality' application for smart phones that enables image-driven browsing. See a garment you like? Then hold your smart phone or tablet computer up to it. If it's stocked by Net-a-Porter, the app will recognise it and all relevant information (including sound and video) will appear on your screen. And you'll be able to buy it instantly. Net-a-Porter knows how to engage internet shoppers like no other fashion retailer. Regular users are quickly hooked: 'Every time those black boxes turn up at the door I feel special,' says Lucy Yeomans. 'Every time I see them I get a little kick.'[18]

---

17 Wiseman, E. (2010) 'One-click wonder: the rise of Net-a-Porter', *The Observer*, 11 July.
18 Wiseman, E. (2010) 'One-click wonder: the rise of Net-a-Porter', *The Observer*, 11 July.

By the end of the first decade of the twenty-first century, marketers were waking up to the fact that consumers were leaving them behind. If they were to stand a chance of reengaging with their customers, marketers would have to learn to speak their language and get comfortable with the lines of communication they were increasingly using. This has meant getting down with their customers and establishing a platform in the virtual world, where the interface of innumerable social networking sites, blogs and wikis had created an unprecedented level of information sharing. Among all the noise, there are invaluable nuggets of knowledge to be found, and among all the activity, real work is being done.

> 'By the end of the first decade of the twenty-first century, marketers were waking up to the fact that consumers were leaving them behind.'

An article in *The Wall Street Journal*[19] in 2008 looked at ways in which marketers were using Web 2.0 tools to engage their customers in novel ways: working with them to refine the marketing process, motivating them to participate, encouraging cross-boundary conversations, inviting consumer innovation. One technology company, for example, created wikis to deal with customers' questions and found that the customers themselves began to contribute significant information and suggestions for product improvement, which the company adopted. Other companies allowed the people contributing to forums on their websites to talk among themselves about unrelated topics – 'That way the site isn't all about the company, it's also about them'. Online communities were created to address specific ideas. In one consumer electronics firm nearly 50,000 people contributed to a product development and marketing forum, using it both to let the company know what they wanted and to suggest innovative ways of providing it. The company lost no time developing prototypes based on their input and the response from the community was instantaneous: 'Members asked when they would be able to buy the products and if they would get the first opportunity to buy them. They didn't have to be sold on anything.'

Today's consumers are actively involved in the innovation and marketing processes adopted by manufacturers. This is what we term the Lego model of marketing and it leads to much more complex marketing planning and execution. It has huge implications for modern marketing organisations, which must be able to engage with customers at multiple touch-points rather than one

---

19 Parise, S., Guinan, P.J. and Weinberg, B.D. (2008) 'The secrets of marketing in a Web 2.0 World', *Wall Street Journal*, 15 December (last accessed 3 March 2012).

key product message. Given the interactive nature of communications today, a brand cannot be a 'finished product'; it must be set up for consumers to create their own interpretation of the brand and what it means to them. Companies now have to fight for the consumer every day, not just every three years as their predecessors did.

This is not a comfortable position to be in: it means redefining a marketing platform and the means to deliver it. Most big global companies shy away from the challenge for two reasons: first, it would mean writing off decades of investment in existing methods and organisations; second, it would mean rejecting the mass media-oriented brand management paradigm that has been good enough for more than a century but (as we will show later) has probably become the single biggest obstacle to marketing innovation. But uncomfortable as this is, there is no other solution to the problems facing FMCG companies than to create new innovation strategies that will permanently refresh and add value to brands and products. These strategies are complex but they must be affordable enough to execute on a global basis. We can learn how to do it by understanding advances in technology and observing some rather unlikely exemplars such as the luxury brands.

> 'Today, a brand cannot be a "finished product"; it must be set up for consumers to create their own interpretation of the brand and what it means to them.'

Chapter 3
From FMCGs to FICGs: Bridging the Innovation Gap

How Brand Strategy Can Undermine Innovation

As we have already seen, brands have a great deal of power and global brands are the life-blood of the big traditional FMCG companies. Not surprisingly these companies are fiercely protective of their brands and constantly alert to anything that could damage, dilute or compromise them. To manage a brand effectively you need a brand strategy that allows you to define, promote and maintain the brand. But brand strategies have themselves to be manageable and all too often they are so rigid that they inhibit innovation and prevent the company from exploiting the potential of the brand to its fullest extent. Afraid to tinker with a proven formula, many companies prefer to milk the brand for all its worth rather than try and add value by innovating around the brand itself.

Really successful brands often become synonymous with their generic product category – thus people might 'Hoover' with an Electrolux vacuum cleaner and a builder might excavate a hole with a 'JCB' that is actually made

'Brand strategies are all too often so rigid that they inhibit innovation and prevent the company from exploiting the potential of the brand to its fullest extent.'

by Terex or Case and not, in fact, by the eponymous UK manufacturer. When brand identity is so strong it often describes what and how such a product should be. For decades Nescafé, for example, let it be known that its immensely successful instant coffee defined how coffee should be – and because other brands were different, Nescafé claimed the advantage. But having put out that message, Nescafé then found it very difficult to innovate: anything new or different clearly wasn't going to be 'how coffee should be' and although the company had plenty of new ideas, spanning this credibility gap was a real challenge. It was only when the competition started to bring out variations on their own premier products and Nestlé itself launched a completely different coffee concept, Nespresso, that the company felt secure enough to launch products such as Nescafé Cuban, Gold and Green. The inhibiting factor here was brand strategy – and it's a common problem. Being a brand manager means you are not an innovator; you might even be anti-innovation. It is rumoured that one leading mobile phone manufacturer actually had a design for a smart phone several years before the first Blackberries and iPhones appeared – but that it shelved the product for fear that it would damage the brand and as a result lost its position in the market.

Jimmi Rembiszewski saw brand strategy limit the full potential of a brand during his time at Procter & Gamble (P&G) in the late 1980s. This occurred shortly after P&G merged with Richardson Vicks and took over a number of products and brands to form a new personal care division:

> I was in a senior marketing role in the company's UK branch and was based at the old Richardson Vicks offices in Egham, west of London, which later became the European headquarters for the personal care division. There were some great brands and products within the Richardson Vicks portfolio, notably Oil of Olay and Clearasil, and there were some dormant products too. One of these was a tonic to prevent male hair loss named Pantene, a name that evolved into the biggest hair care brand in the world. There were also several underexploited baby products, including shampoos and associated bath care products, marketed under the Infacare name and the Milton brand of sterilising products. I saw huge potential in these brands and promoted the idea of developing a whole range of baby products under the Pampers umbrella – baby shampoo, baby bath, body lotion, soothing creams and even sterilising equipment – which I proposed relaunching as the Pampers–Milton system. Pampers, at that time, was narrowly positioned as a superior brand of disposable diaper but its popularity offered a good platform for a broader range of baby care products.

> The principle behind my idea was very simple – to extend the Pampers brand strategy to 'Pampers: The Ultimate in Baby Care'. This new umbrella strategy would allow us to stretch the Pampers brand value to incorporate all kinds of care products that, individually, would generate a very lucrative margin. All baby products tend to have higher prices and higher margins. Once these new products were introduced into the home, they would be used by everyone in the family, because of Pampers' special care connotation: if it's good enough for a baby's skin or hair, it must be good enough for everybody. Even better was the pay-off that Pampers diapers would get from the extended line, which would help the diapers steal a march over the competition, which attacked Pampers' position as the number one diaper with various product innovations and price cuts. It would be a win–win all around. The core diapers business would benefit from a broadening and deepening of its brand image while the new line

would increase customer awareness; and we would also create a new range of baby products using product technology we'd inherited from the merger. I thought it was a multi-billion dollar slam-down. We could use the Pampers brand as a launch platform for new products and innovation, taking advantage of the well-established Pampers hospital sampling, where every newborn received a free gift selection of Pampers products. I was already thinking in the long term, projecting ahead to bringing out a line of Pampers baby food products. When I presented this idea to my bosses at Procter & Gamble I was laughed out of court. The response was, 'Jimmi, Pampers is in the paper division. It stands for comfort, hygiene and dryness. What the hell does baby shampoo have to do with this?' And that was that. Later P&G did expand the Pampers brand into other products, including baby wipes, but the brand still remains very narrowly within the sanitary-wear sector and after 20 years there is still no Pampers shampoo, bath and shower gel, cream or sterilising product on the market.

The problem was that P&G was stuck in the past with a brand strategy that was no longer fit for purpose and certainly not about to innovate. P&G was one of the greatest marketing innovators of the twentieth century and generations of marketers have grown up on brand-building principles devised by the company nearly a century ago. The P&G philosophy is a highly disciplined, three-paragraph brand or copy strategy.

The first paragraph defined the brand essentials, or key brand benefits, which could be dramatised in TV and radio commercials, on hoardings, in magazine advertisements and so on. The copy or strategy was debated and analysed for months on end by the entire senior management group and their agencies until the content and wording were perfect. Most of the time this was marketing-led, although occasionally it was led by product innovation if there was a very strong drive from R&D management. This first paragraph established the product's basic positioning, for example, 'Ariel cleans better at lower temperatures'.

After the definition of the brand, the second, or support, paragraph defined why the consumer should believe the product promise. 'Why does Ariel clean better at lower temperatures? Because only Ariel has the special ingredient...' Typically, product demonstrations in the middle of TV ads would show Persil washing whiter, or in other sectors, would show that Cadbury's Dairy Milk chocolate contained a pint and a half of full cream milk, or that Jack Daniels tasted better because of the slow process involved in distilling it. This template endured for more than 60 years.

The final paragraph defined the tone of voice or character of the brand and how it was communicated. Other elements could be enshrined in this actual or virtual third paragraph and over time these could become essential elements of the brand identity. For example, from a uniquely televisual aspect, every Lenor advertisement would show the slow-motion drop of the fabric conditioner bottle into a basket of soft laundry that folded round it. We all wait for the last line of the L'Oréal advertisement – 'Because you're worth it'; and some images became so iconic that no words were needed to project the character of the brand – the Marlboro cowboy, the Coca-Cola bottle.

The P&G approach to brand building was adopted across the entire FMCG industry and was copied by generations of agencies and their clients on the basis of this three-paragraph brief: benefit, reason why and brand character. The best examples did not change their strategy for decades; campaigns might be refreshed two or three times a year but the key benefits stayed the same. The key principles were that the brand benefits were true, based on demonstrable product testing and competitive edge, and that the message would be reinforced, rather than worn out, by changing (principally television) advertising.

A lot of work from the entire senior management team went into the wording of these strategic documents and the entire R&D effort was exhausted with trying to keep the strategic product benefit ahead of the competition. This meant that every three years R&D had to come up with an on-strategy innovation, giving consumers the reasons to justify a high price while maintaining the basic brand strategy and its key elements of execution relatively unchanged.

This three-year cycle was enough to keep consumers engaged without the risk of alienating them by changing the brand beyond recognition. We are not deriding this model – but neither are we endorsing it. It certainly isn't working today, but why?

'TV commercials and print advertising compete today with instant messaging and instant exchanges through networking sites like Facebook that are updated literally every minute of the day.'

The first reason is that twenty-first century consumers are very different from the two generations of consumer that preceded them. They expect much more than a well-communicated end benefit that beats a competing product by a very narrow definition. The new consumer just wants the 'latest', so each innovation has to add to or improve the key benefit of the product. These consumers know when somebody's giving them a sales patter and they don't like to be patronised. Therefore marketers have to challenge modern consumers' scepticism about marketing and address the real value that customers expect to get from the products they buy. Today, consumers are much more cynical about advertising; simple advertisements don't work any more and the return on them has declined dramatically. Using traditional advertising, particularly ads that focus on celebrity endorsement, suggests that advertisers have run out of ideas and are heading for the innovation gap. Teenagers especially see through old campaign constructions and so even the most sophisticated, entertaining or amusing executions wear out almost instantly. TV commercials and print advertising compete today with instant messaging and instant exchanges through networking sites like Facebook that are updated literally every minute of the day. More importantly, these networks carry greater credibility with this new breed of consumer than any form of advertising because it is generated by real people and their friends.

This is not a new phenomenon. Product history is littered with examples of companies that failed to connect with young consumers. For example, the confectionery manufacturer Hershey and instant coffee producer Maxwell House could have captured the European market after the Second World War. These companies (both American) had kept US forces supplied with chocolate and instant coffee while they were overseas. In fact, Hershey produced a 125g bar of non-melting chocolate that formed part of troops' field rations; packing 600 calories, it was designed to keep the men going when there was no other food available. Hershey's factory was turned over to the war effort and at one point was producing half a million bars of chocolate a day. At the end of the war, both Hershey and Maxwell House brands had acquired a high profile on a continent struggling with several years of strict rationing. As the saying goes, 'The Yanks arrived with chocolate and left with British brides.' Yet neither brand pressed home its advantage; both missed the open goal of a European market for their products because they were too wedded to their preconceived ideas about the demands of their typical customers.

The second reason why the old twentieth century brand strategies no longer work has to do with the economic and technical challenges of coming up with ground-breaking innovations of the key benefits. Demonstrating a clear competitive product advantage to an apathetic consumer base in what has become a generic product category takes a lot of time, a lot of R&D and a lot of manufacturing investment. In the motor industry you can understand an R&D cycle of three to five years simply because of the need for huge investments in technology and manufacturing infrastructure. But for everyday products like detergents, personal care products, food and drink, long innovation cycles lead to disaster and only generate price competition and the growth of generic own brands.

'The inability to bring innovations to everyday products faster and more cheaply has put enormous pressure on price to justify the higher costs of development.'

Thirty years ago a product upgrade of Pampers diapers could cost more than £100 million. If you add to this an extensive and costly testing programme followed by a global roll-out, you get into very substantial and risky investments that require a significant uplift of brand sales to pay for them. The inability to bring innovations to everyday products faster and more cheaply has put enormous pressure on price to justify the higher costs of development. Because innovation cycles have grown longer and longer, and consumers have moved away from branded products, the big consumer goods companies have tried to battle with trade incentives, new variations of the same message (usually with more production values added), and the use of celebrities to endorse products. The logical consequence of this is more and more cost pressure and more spending on non-consumer relevant parts of the value chain.

The third reason for the failure of the old brand strategy model is that some of these core product benefits have reached such a degree of saturation that today's consumers are unimpressed by small incremental improvements in the brand's core qualities and certainly don't consider them a reason for paying more. Who cares whether there is a detergent that cleans more thoroughly or gets your whites even whiter if the cleanliness and whiteness it already achieves more than satisfies your expectations? Thirty years ago the word 'New!' emblazoned on packs was guaranteed to boost sales; but such terms rely on credibility, which is finite. The twenty-first-century consumer no longer accepts that 'new' is a good enough reason to switch brands or buy more product.

A long innovation cycle and the high cost of product innovations for improving key brand benefits are the core reasons why many of the world's leading FMCG companies are suffering, especially in highly developed economies. Competition from generic brands creates additional pressure and the FMCGs respond by reducing prices – doing just this gave Marlboro a place in marketing folklore, for the wrong reasons.

In the early 1990s something very worrying happened for Philip Morris: cheaper brands of cigarette started to take a larger share of the domestic market and Marlboro found itself losing sales. This was no blip on the graph; it was a gathering trend and the crisis point finally came on Friday, 2 April 1993 – a day that has gone down in marketing history as 'Marlboro Friday' – when Philip Morris announced that it was cutting the price of Marlboro cigarettes by 20 per cent in a bid to head off the competition.

The impact on the market and investors was massive. Philip Morris shares plummeted 26 per cent and started a wave of stock market write-downs: not only did rival tobacco giant British American Tobacco (BAT) see its stock fall 15 per cent in response, but several other famous brands entirely unrelated to the tobacco industry, including Coca-Cola, Procter & Gamble and Disney, also saw their share price fall.

Philip Morris's actions on Marlboro Friday sent out a powerful message to consumers: the leader had faltered; it had lost its nerve; it was no longer leader of the pack. The brand image was destroyed.

Analysts were quick to conclude that companies that relied heavily on the strength of their brands were severely weakened. Brands were no longer good enough to see off low-cost commodity products and it began to look as if high-end companies could no longer justify their premium prices. The future belonged to whoever could churn out products at the lowest price.

The evidence was certainly there to back up the theory. Only a week or two before Marlboro Friday, Kellogg, P&G and Heinz all published results showing massive falls in profit margin. The crisis was not confined to the US either. In the UK, Tomkins Plc, the conglomerate that had acquired food giant Rank Hovis McDougall (RHM) the previous autumn, announced that it was writing off the £600 million at which RHM had valued its brands. This was highly significant because during the 1980s RHM had been one of the first to put a balance-sheet value on its brands, which included Hovis, Bisto and Mr Kipling cakes.

Marlboro Man's fall from grace made people question their belief in the value of brands. If Marlboro could not sustain its position and demand a premium price, then no other premium brand could. Marlboro Friday swept away existing preconceptions and many people in the marketing industry believe that it changed the dynamics of consumer marketing forever.

The fall-out from Marlboro Friday left many believing that henceforth price was king: consumers would always be attracted to the most competitively-priced products and refuse to pay a premium price for a particular brand.

'Many people in the marketing industry believe that Marlboro Friday changed the dynamics of consumer marketing forever.'

That explains why these companies have moved more and more into value proposition, offering high-quality, lower-priced products themselves, creating huge margin pressure from a high cost base, to compete against companies with a very low cost base.

'Companies often cannibalise their premium, top-of-the-range brands with their own low-price products.'

The situation is unwinnable and, worse, reduces the ability to innovate even further. These companies often cannibalise their premium, top-of-the-range brands with their own low-price products. In stable or declining product categories, this can create a fast downward spiral of profit margin. Trade brands and generics are enjoying a great ride as a result, while for the last few decades the response for FMCGs has been to consolidate to get synergy cost reductions in order to prolong their outdated business model. Markets are saturated in terms of volume and benefits. FMCGs know they need to increase the speed of innovation, but don't know how.

Small, rapid innovations that the customer understands – and how you can make them happen – are key. If companies want to move fast, they come up with a prototype and then improve on it. Nestlé did this with the launch of Nespresso, which we will look at in more detail later in the book. But once again, we need to look at Apple to see how speedy innovation can really improve an existing product. With the iPad, iPhone and iMac, Apple has three very important prototypical platforms for continuing innovation around an original product.

Apple started out as a computer company, of course, and although it quickly earned a reputation for innovation it constantly lagged behind Microsoft, which commanded the lion's share of the desktop computer market. Apple's true genius only became fully apparent with the launch of the iPod in 2001. Combining the relatively new MP3 audio technology for personal digital devices with Apple's skill at designing intuitive user interfaces, the iPod caused a sensation with its claim to be able to 'put 1,000 songs in your pocket'.

To support the new device, Apple introduced iTunes, a computer programme for downloading, playing and organising music files on desktop computers and media players. By making the iPod compatible only with the Apple operating system, Apple ensured that the iPod was never a one-off purchase: users had to get their music downloads from iTunes and hence continued to spend money with Apple after purchasing their device.

The iPod's phenomenal success quickly outgrew other personal digital media and while selling the devices as quickly as it could make them, Apple also enjoyed a fast-growing market for downloads via the online iTunes Store. While sales of devices and downloads grew strongly, Apple soon added another string to its bow. Just as it had cornered the market for MP3 players, Apple now addressed the emerging smart phone sector with another best-in-class product: the iPhone.

Cellular telephony was new to Apple. The sector was already dominated by a handful of big and very powerful operators including Nokia, Sony-Ericsson and Vodafone and there was not much room in the market for a new player. But Apple's superior expertise in software development, graphical user interfaces and internet applications gave it a head-start in the new multifunction smart phone sector.

Apple boss Steve Jobs unveiled the original iPhone in January 2007. Then, after six months of carefully orchestrated hype, the device finally went on sale amid scenes of such hysterical excitement that some commentators started to refer to it as 'the Jesus phone'.

With its built-in MP3 player, the iPhone gave Apple customers another reason to buy downloads from the iTunes store and sales of music downloads grew accordingly. But smart phones – as the name indicates – are capable of many functions. The iPhone, for example, can function as a camera phone, video camera, portable media player and internet client with email and web-browsing capabilities. It can send text messages and receive visual voicemail and has both Wifi and 3G connectivity.

The iPhone is an excellent example of the 'Lego' marketing principle: a multifaceted, multi-feature, multi-benefit device allowing constant innovation on many levels in some or all of them. Even better, the product is being continuously renewed by the almost daily addition of new applications, or 'apps' – pieces of software that users can download and which perform a variety of functions such as computer games, GPS navigation programmes, social networking and business applications. Some apps are available free of charge but most are sold. The majority are also engineered by independent third parties and the income from those that are not free is usually split between the producer and the distributor. Typically, 30 per cent of the cost of a third-party iPhone or iPod app goes to iTunes.

Apple has capitalised on the sale of apps not just for its iPhone but also for its latest generation of iPods. While the original iPod was a single-function device (it played music) the latest iPod Touch is a portable media player, personal digital assistant, handheld games console and Wifi mobile device for internet browsing and emailing. Apple boss Steve Jobs called the iPod Touch 'training wheels for the iPhone', which it closely resembles in appearance and with which it shares most of its software. Apps can add value to the iPod Touch in a way music downloads cannot.

It is no surprise therefore that Apple has ploughed a lot of money and effort into building up the App Store. Apps are cheaper than songs and, unlike music downloads, many apps are free so there are few iPhone and iPod users who do not use them. In October 2011, Apple released its latest download figures, enabling analysts to compare music downloads with apps. They found that the total number of apps downloaded overtook music downloads for the first time in June 2011. By October, the rate of downloads for Apps hit one billion per month, or roughly 34 million per day, whereas the corresponding rate for songs was less than 8.5 million per day.

In terms of revenue, music downloads still contribute more than apps simply because so many apps are free. In 2011, analyst Asymco calculated that Apple's monthly income from music downloads was currently $80 million and from apps around $75 million. But the App Store only started trading in September 2008, whereas iTunes first went on sale four years previously and it would only be a matter of time before the revenue from apps overtook the revenue from music downloads. 'At a billion downloads a month (and rising) the [apps] value in terms of revenues is already a run rate of $2.9 billion per year. This has been enough to overtake a business [music] that has been running for more than seven years,' concluded Asymco.[1]

However it is not just about bottom-line revenues. The growth in app downloads drives sales of Apple's most popular products. 'The value to Apple of apps versus music is less about pure revenues, and much more about what's selling more hardware. With apps a much bigger factor in selling iPhones, iPod touches and iPads than songs, the App Store arguably superseded the iTunes Store in corporate value to Apple long ago,' comments digital music business information and strategy company Music Ally.com.[2]

---

1   Dediu, H. (2011) 'At $2.9bn/yr apps are challenging songs as the most valuable online medium', www.asymco.com, 6 October.
2   Music Ally (2011) 'Apps catching up to songs in value for Apple', www.musically.com, 7 October (accessed 20 February 2014).

The Innovation Gap

FMCGs need to recognise that there is a direct correlation between the lack of innovation and lower margins. This is what we call the innovation gap, the space in which faster-innovating competitors can steal in and take market share, forcing the slower-innovating FMCGs to drop prices and squeeze margins.

Newness can no longer be measured in spans of three to four years. The threshold of newness is now very short – about six months – and the rhythm of innovation has changed because of consumer expectations. The story behind Apple's App Store is the perfect example of how continuous innovation and product enhancement can be achieved. And although it's not the sort of innovation most FMCGs would expect to deliver, they have to find a way.

However, FMCGs are almost invariably tumbling into the innovation gap. In the typical old-fashioned FMCG, slow-moving innovators are locked into the benefits of brands that have steadily become generic. They spend a lot of time improving things that modern consumers perceive as irrelevant – a whiter or cleaner wash, less dandruff, fresher drink and so on. Modern consumers are cannier and hungrier and their expectations are fed by what they learn from industries that are more relevant to their lifestyle – fashion, smart phones, the internet, music, film and social networking.

But what does the innovation gap look like? Figure 3.1 shows two different innovation curves. The upper curve represents traditional, large, expensive, longer term upgrades; the flatter curve below illustrates smaller but faster improvements of new features or, in the case of umbrella brands, new line extensions. The space between these two curves is the innovation gap.

The innovation gap will lead a company into loss of market share, or margin erosion or both. Assuming a normal cost inflation of 3 to 5 per cent, you need to increase consumer prices in line with this just to stand still. Thirty years ago this pressure could be compensated for by volume, but in today's saturated western markets volume is declining. If nothing happens to improve the offer and the competition does not follow this price increase, the premium brand market share will come under the kind of pressure that FMCGs typically try to compensate for by price reductions.

So price increases are accompanied by loss of market share or an inflated promotions budget with temporary price offers. This equates to reduction in margins. To make things worse, price offers are directly positioned against

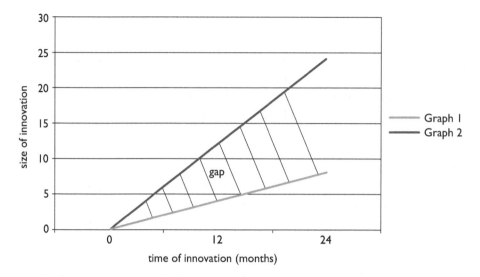

Figure 3.1   The innovation gap

branded products. Producers of generics, with no names or trade brands, will be
able to offer similar products at a much lower price and grab significant market
share during the innovation gap. The response of FMCGs is to launch their
own low-price brands and add even more pressure to their premium brands.

> 'Producers of generics will be able to
> offer similar products at a much lower
> price and grab significant market
> share during the innovation gap.'

Unsurprisingly this has brought
about a significant, even explosive,
growth in the value-for-money
segments – from 10 per cent to 50 per
cent of the market. These offers can
afford much lower margins because they
have no overhead, no R&D costs and no own production because, ironically,
FMCGs have so much overcapacity that they gladly manufacture not only their
own low-price offers but also trade brands and others.

Thus we see an unholy spiral of cost inflation, full consumer price increase,
loss of market share and lower margins on full-priced brand offers. This
relationship is shown in Figure 3.2. The lower curve is the ideal price increase
line, going up with inflation and keeping margins constant. The upper curve is
the actual line, with lower price increases due to market dynamics.

In a lot of markets, mainly in the developed world, we see companies
that have tried to mount huge cost-saving programmes through lower-cost
manufacturing, productivity gains from product harmonisation, and moving to
low-cost locations in the developing world. This leads to more homogeneity in

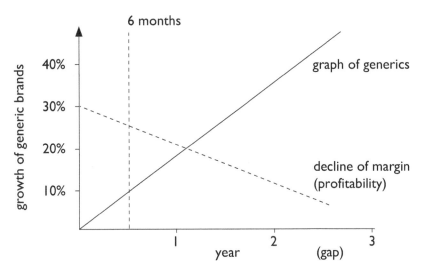

Figure 3.2   The negation effect on margin

products, further reducing the differentiation of premium brands from budget brands. Another move is market consolidation, leading to bigger companies using the new scale for temporary productivity gains. All these are short-term measures and do not represent a sustainable model.

We believe the only sustainable long-term strategy is to close the innovation gap with faster innovation cycles that offer consumers relevant improvements and reduce the space available for low-priced offers. To do this we

> 'The only sustainable long-term strategy is to close the innovation gap with faster innovation cycles.'

need a new model, a new way of marketing that allows us to compete with products that are proven winners in the twenty-first century – products that have a much more flexible strategy definition, create new consumer demand through faster and novel innovation, and do so within six months rather than three years. And this model can be found in sectors where FMCGs are unlikely to look for inspiration. Many are from the technology sector but not all by any means; the tobacco industry provides some outstanding examples.

A classic deadlocked rivalry existed between BAT and Philip Morris, producers of the world's leading cigarette brand, Marlboro. BAT could only compete against the incumbent with flexibility and fast innovations. Philip Morris found it hard to compete with these fast changes because the company was well entrenched and had 'perfected' its product and marketing over the decades. Jimmi Rembiszewski analyses the strategic challenge between Phillip Morris and BAT:

When I joined part of the then very diversified BAT group as a marketing director in 1991 the world's tobacco industry was host to numerous powerful companies, each with a strong local presence in its chosen markets. But there was only one dominant global player and that was Phillip Morris. I don't think any company had ever dominated a world market the way Phillip Morris did the tobacco market. And much of that domination was down to having something that all the other players aspired to – a global premium brand: Marlboro.

For decades Phillip Morris has focused obsessively on this one brand. As soon as Marlboro became the leading brand in the USA the company launched the identical model all over the world – the same product (described in the industry jargon as a 'US blend style filter product'), the same pack design, the same premium price and same marketing support evoking the iconic cowboy image. This archetypical American symbol became more than the holy grail of the tobacco industry; together with Coca-Cola it was one of the world's most valuable global brands. Marlboro was revered in marketing circles as the supreme example of consistency in brand building over decades, repeating the same big picture and product. Consumers never seemed to tire of it and the product, pack and marketing support were only marginally updated over decades.

This resulted in a stronghold in virtually all the markets in the world. Even in markets where Phillip Morris arrived late, and where BAT or other players had leadership positions, the company launched Marlboro and stuck stubbornly to the formula. It persevered even where consumers didn't like the product, or had a hostile attitude towards the US – during the Vietnam War, for example. It was a question of belief: the corporate mantra was that if it worked in the USA market, it had to work everywhere else. Anyone in the Phillip Morris Company who expressed scepticism about this was seen as traitor.

In some markets it took Phillip Morris many years to become successful. But it got there in the end. It had everything it needed to succeed: the leading brand, a premium price, the most desirable product and the most valuable smokers (that is, those in their twenties).

Because everything was dictated from the US centre, Philip Morris could optimise all the elements down to the production process. Procurement worked on a global basis, including leaf buying and production of a standard product and pack, and marketing support was virtually standard for all the markets. New versions of the cowboy ads were used around the world. Altogether, it was an awesome money machine; Marlboro commanded the highest prices at the lowest costs. From all business perspectives, it was paradise for Phillip Morris. Consistency allowed it to optimise this machine year on year. And since all its competitors tried to follow with similar offers its leadership was legitimised even more.

BAT's position at that time (that is, the early 1990s) could not have been more different. BAT had been built up over almost a century by a series of local acquisitions around the world. It had a presence in more than 150 markets, each built around a distinctive local brand and product portfolio. Until the early 1980s BAT was the world's largest global tobacco company but it had been losing ground to Phillip Morris for decades.

BAT was an international company with no global approach. When the Berlin Wall fell and the world started to open up, BAT even began competing with itself as its constituent companies started to explore emerging markets with their own local brands. With its highly diversified portfolio of local, lower-priced brands, BAT had higher costs, much lower margins and declining market shares compared with Philip Morris and the company was in trouble.

Like all of Phillip Morris's competitors, BAT was busy trying to come up with something similar to Marlboro in terms of US-style and marketing positioning. It was spending more time and money on re-engineering the Marlboro model than improving its own products.

In terms of tobacco market segmentation and outlook, the accepted wisdom was that the world was divided into brands that could grow (US-style products and US heritage) and all the rest. The latter included UK-style blends and brands that used to be preferred in the British Commonwealth but which were in terminal decline.

In the mid-1990s, BAT started to develop a tobacco strategy that it could own, which was built to its strengths and would be very difficult for Phillip Morris to follow – provided it worked. We needed to turn the tables and redefine the rules of the tobacco marketing game. Most managers in BAT could not see the point. Why not accept BAT's strong, profitable number two position in the world market and manage the company on its historic strengths: local lower-price brands with the odd regional addition of some international brands, of which it had plenty?

Others, however, thought differently. Martin Broughton, then chairman of BAT, and some new board members – including Paul Adams, who joined with me in 1991, having worked in international consumer product companies – supported a new BAT strategy: how can you argue with the ambition to become number one? Nevertheless, a lot of senior managers and management board members did. They thought the new strategy was unrealistic and could become dangerously destructive. And given that

BAT was so diversified, not only in terms of product but also in its corporate structure, anything developed at the centre as a global strategy would not be easy to execute at the outer reaches of the organisation.

We started by defining a brand strategy that would not be built around a Marlboro-type one-size-fits-all approach nor would follow traditional product segmentation such as US-style blend versus UK-style but would give our portfolio of brands real differentiation in all aspects of their positioning. This would allow us to define future product and format innovations for these brands, again moving away from creating a model based on consistency of brand expression.

We identified four brands that would constitute a global brand portfolio which we could implement in all markets around the world. They were Kent, Pall Mall, Lucky Strike and Dunhill (from 1999, after the merger with Rothmans). None of them had the right positioning at the time, none had a global presence and – even worse – all of them had a pedigree of decline in their traditional positioning. With the exception of a few markets they were all seen as very old and tired, with no real relevance to smokers in their twenties. But in their new definition they were very different from each other: each would be redefined as a different product and have a different marketing strategy, so they could all compete in the same market and would, if successful, carve out different segments. Most importantly, they were all very different from our competitors.

With this strategy, we believed that Phillip Morris would have to respond in one of two ways: either develop new brands or do the unthinkable and stretch the Marlboro brand itself. This would mean challenging the core values that had been absorbed and implemented by all Phillip Morris markets and departments for decades, and destroying the masterminded global simplicity of the single global brand. Any disruption would increase the cost and complexity of their model. So if the new strategy worked for BAT, it would be poison for Phillip Morris.

However, the perfect beauty of this strategy had one major drawback; in the first six or seven years it showed no sign of working. Our global market share continued to slip and Phillip Morris got stronger, especially in the new markets of Eastern Europe. It seemed that all smokers wanted Marlboro. Obviously, this was proof to the many sceptics in BAT that the new strategy had been doomed to fail from the start. And my position as marketing director in the early 2000s became increasingly difficult.

In addition to putting a lot of money behind the four new global brands, we also started developing product innovations; these were not only expensive to develop but also challenged our manufacturing organisation, which wanted to bring the cost down and to synergise as many blends and sizes as possible.

Finally, we started to revolutionise our route to market. In an industry that is barred from using mass media and must target adult consumers, the point of purchase is critical. As a consequence we developed a trade marketing strategy wholly integrated into the marketing organisation. There would be no more separation between marketing and sales, as is still the case in most organisations. Consumer marketing, trade marketing, insight and innovation became one very consumer-focused activity.

To be able to communicate with smokers using only the point of purchase we developed a direct selling operation. In markets where most goods were sold via distributors, wholesalers and organised retail organisations, we went direct to the retailer and delivered the goods. This added another layer of cost and capital to our organisation. But it allowed us to control how our products were displayed and use the retailer to explain certain product innovations to the smoker.

This made the strategy even more attractive – assuming it worked – but it was still not showing great signs of success. Even those who had supported me and the strategy for quite a while started to express their doubts and my position became pretty weak. Nevertheless, we carried on – maybe because of the lack of a suitable alternative but perhaps also because there were some signs in some markets that the brands and strategy could work. Then in 2003–4 it all started to come together.

Once the message had filtered through to the customer, our strategy started to deliver results. Today the global brands show constant growth every year, outpacing our competitors significantly; all four have true global presence and are multi-billion dollar brands. BAT has performed like no other FMCG company in the last decade. Total shareholder return is excellent and very much based on sustainable global value creation.

The portfolio approach, with constant innovations, has successfully challenged Philip Morris's one product, one pack, big picture model, making BAT today a real leader.

I don't know how they managed it, but the people responsible for the 1950s made a world in which pretty much everything was good for you. Drinks before dinner? The more the better! Smoke? You bet! ... 'Just what the doctor ordered!' read ads for L&M cigarettes ... By the end of the decade the American consumer could choose from nearly 100 brands of ice cream, five hundred types of breakfast cereals and nearly as many makes of coffee.[3]

---

3   Bryson, B. (2007) *The Life and Times of the Thunderbolt Kid*, London, Black Swan.

Making Room for Innovation

There is simply no room in the global market today for the cornucopia of small brands that Bill Bryson remembers so nostalgically. We are forced to recognise now that sometimes the cost of keeping old brands alive is too high. But how do you get old brands to die faster and make room for innovations without losing the connection to the consumer? The BAT story demonstrates one method, migrating an existing product into a newly branded one.

The core to the problem is the underlying brand or marketing strategy. We have to get rid of the outdated idea of striving for the end benefit as the *non plus ultra* of a brand, which required lengthy interrogations of ideas to check whether or not they were on-strategy improvements. As we have already shown, FMCGs have built their marketing strategies and organisations around what was safe and worked in the past. These they have optimised until they have become very efficient in-house marketing factories. With the help of numerous consultants, they have streamlined and benchmarked all elements, from personnel to creative briefs to agency contracts – all with the help of modern procurement and with the ambition to have the lowest-cost marketing on the planet. The result is that all these efforts have gone towards optimising an inherently ineffective organisation.

This isn't the way to transform a company into an FICG fit to meet the new challenges of fast innovations, global roll-out speed and a platform for new, complex brand building. Innovating companies offer consumers surprises, news, excitement, features and extensions of well-known brands that significantly improve the overall value to them. The smaller, younger companies tend to be much better at providing a faster innovation cycle to the consumer, improving the total offer on a 6–12-month cycle in which the price increases but not without giving something back to the consumer to justify upping the price.

> 'Innovating companies offer consumers surprises, news, excitement, features and extensions of well-known brands.'

The Apple iPhone topped it all. Each revamped version has come packed with new and better features except an improvement to the core benefit – better quality phone calls – and the price has remained very high. Each new iPhone generates very real consumer excitement – and most of the consumers who queue for days to get one already have the earlier model. These are the dynamics that traditional FMCGs have to study as the new model for twenty-first century marketing because this is the level of innovation that modern consumers expect from all their brands.

The tobacco industry is highly innovative in its marketing – but because it is tobacco, it has a much lower profile than other sectors. Today's tobacco industry is characterised by a global race of new products, features and line extensions. As we saw earlier, 20 years ago BAT was a company with global presence but no global brands. Then, in the space of 15 years, BAT built four truly global brands from existing brands with great heritage and name recognition: Dunhill, Kent, Lucky Strike and Pall Mall. How did they do it? By finding a way to speed up the innovation cycle and capture the attention of the consumer, despite a number of internal and external hurdles.

Kent is one of the biggest success stories at BAT and involved the successful migration of an old, 'irrelevant' brand into a truly global brand. Kent was repositioned with technology because that was what key consumer was interested in. Initially, people in the company had a problem with technology. Instinctively, they wanted to put 'heart' into Kent, and create the kind of emotional brand loyalty that Phillip Morris's Marlboro had harnessed so successfully. But as the unassailable position of Marlboro in the market had shown, it is hard to create an emotional relationship between brand and consumer. It's far easier to build on a rational, technological proposition, for example, a new filter, new packaging, different strengths. It might be expensive, but it is more sustainable and less fickle or subjective.

Repositioning the brand using technology meant that a new innovation was needed every six months, and that had to be planned ahead. Every meeting to plan innovation addressed the 'So what?' question: a better type of packaging – so what? The critical thing was to discover the 'meaning' consumers would ascribe to the new technology – for example, a better type of packaging means that their cigarettes no longer fall out and crumble in their handbag. Appearance was crucial: lean, hi-tech packaging meant the cigarettes would fit well next to the smoker's iPod in a handbag or pocket. The cigarette itself was resized and became smaller, with one-third less tobacco but a higher price. This strategy generated a significant amount of profit. Then came the question of achieving global reach for the revamped brand.

It is very hard to introduce a new brand to a market. The key is to create awareness and consumer loyalty. The launch of a premium brand could take as long as 20 years and if successful might reach a small market share. Also, engineers don't like brand launches with new formats. This is because their machines had been amortised long ago for the production of an established brand; production of a new version of the brand would mean writing off billions in machinery and investing in more. Hence a global launch of 'new Kent' would have been prohibitively expensive. However, changes in manufacturing become more affordable if they can be financed by revenue from existing products. BAT's answer was to leverage existing old-fashioned, local franchises as a launch pad for their new modern strategic global brands.

The first example was Barclay, already a strong local brand in some parts of Europe. Barclay was simply renamed Kent; the market adjusted quickly to the name change because the product remained the same. In due course, however, the product was changed to new Kent, bringing it into line with the revamped brand and automatically increasing its global footprint. From start to finish, this migration took eight years, much less time than launching and growing a new brand to the same level of sales.

This innovation platform also helped get BAT out of a pure price competition with its legal and illegal competitors (counterfeit products are a serious threat to the tobacco industry). Counterfeiters do not want to copy a highly innovative product because of the prohibitive manufacturing cost, so they tend to fake simpler products and formats that are easy to copy. It was also a great lesson in the geographic attractiveness of innovative products. Rolling out new brands like Kent ran counter to the old model, which can be summarised as 'promote first to the developed world and the developing world will follow'. To a large degree, it was the other way round with Kent. In western Europe – saturated markets where consumer goods companies have been unable or unwilling to change their marketing model – consumers tend to be much more willing to trade down and buy cheaper. In developing markets, consumers upgrade – the less wealthy need brands to define themselves, while the rich can drive a Porsche but shop at Aldi. Of course, this strategy only works if a brand portfolio is relatively homogenised and innovation can be launched quickly. It's no good doing local innovation then trying to spread because competitors will be after you like a shot.

'In western Europe and the States consumers tend to be much more willing to trade down and buy cheaper. In developing markets, consumers upgrade.'

Umbrella Brands and Luxury Goods

Not all FMCGs have fallen into the same trap of clinging desperately to the outmoded twentieth-century way of doing things. Over the past 20 years there have been some very impressive examples of classic consumer brands successfully bringing this kind of exciting new innovation to market – including some outstanding examples where, within a broader brand strategy, a proposition has been radically updated with very fast innovation cycles. There are many cases of a brand with a tremendous heritage being transplanted from its original narrow category into entirely new markets via line extensions, as Jimmi Rembiszewski proposed doing with Pampers in the late 1980s. These are the 'umbrella brands' – brand houses that, without altering the overarching brand identity, manage to bring in new and often unexpected categories until there's a rich cornucopia of complementary lines all gathered together and sharing the same character and projecting the same successful brand values. They are brands like Nivea, Oil of Olay and L'Oréal in personal care and Nestlé, Milka and Danone in foods. Their parent companies have successfully built mega brands that almost behave as companies in their own right, spreading their brand identity from its originally narrow core definition to all kinds of new product categories. Having broken the shackles of product categorisation, umbrella brands also have the advantage of being able to move easily and quickly to exploit new social trends.

An example of this is Nivea, which has made a very impressive move from the basic product – hand cream – to a range covering almost the entire male and female personal care category. The brand was rejuvenated and made more relevant to a younger consumer market and in the process had billions added to its worth without touching the core product. When was the last relaunch of Nivea hand cream? Even the classic blue-and-white packaging has remained unchanged. Under the umbrella brand, Nivea developed a two-pronged strategy: stable lines with no change to their traditional products, colour or packaging, and rapid innovation in new products.

Milka chocolate has achieved a similar reach. The standard bar of Milka milk chocolate is 100g, a perfect size in market terms but carrying a relatively high price; a standard-sized bar cannot be sold for a higher price so if ingredient prices go up, there is a problem. Milka needed more revenue streams with a high margin. Line extension led to different sizes of bar and products, for example, the 35g Lila Pause, while the traditional 100g tablet was retained. A new offering was brought out every six months without touching the core brand.

Adidas is another example of how to manage an umbrella brand. Starting out with just a single product line – a football boot – it has grown to become a massive brand producing all kinds of sport and leisure shoe plus a full range of fashion items. The heritage line of classic football equipment remains the company's core brand with high-tech running shoes as line extensions. And its customer base in very broad, ranging from the schoolboy kicking a ball about in the park to fashion-conscious adults, and from the German national football team to Madonna. It is hard to imagine that in the 1990s, following its disastrous acquisition by the subsequently discredited French businessman and politician Bernard Tapie, this company came to the brink of bankruptcy. Today it is stronger than ever, vying with Nike for the number one spot in its sector.

Taking a well-established brand that is associated with a limited and clearly defined product range and extending it into new and unfamiliar markets takes a lot of courage – and a lot of skill. However, the unfurling of a successful 'umbrella brand' can add massively to its market value, often at very little risk. Simply repackaging an existing core product to make it attractive to a new market segment can boost sales and bolster brand value.

The process by which an umbrella brand extends its reach tends to be incremental and there is usually a common thread running through the product range, however disparate it becomes. It makes sense, therefore, for a fashion brand to branch out into perfumes and for a confectionery manufacturer to develop a range of desserts or drinks. Few attempt to leap far beyond their familiar territory – as Virgin Group did in the mid-1980s when Richard Branson added air travel to his music publishing portfolio.

Many successful umbrella brands are people – cleverly marketed celebrities with hordes of adoring fans. The number of soap stars, catwalk models and 'reality' TV celebrities who have capitalised on their glitzy image by launching a fragrance or a fashion range are too numerous to mention. But people brands are among the most difficult to transfer to new sectors for the simple reason that their core market tends to be their fan-base, a self-selecting constituency to which all branded products must appeal. Which is why American designer Tom Ford is such a notable exception.

Ford is in the fashion business and always has been attracted to art and design. Born in Texas in 1961, he briefly studied art history at New York University before flunking out and trying his hand at acting in television commercials – tellingly, a business in which he did rather well. After a year or so, Ford returned to education, enrolling at the New School in Greenwich Village to study interior architecture. That, too, was short-lived and Ford interrupted his studies to visit Europe.

His entry into the fashion business came during an 18-month stay in Paris where he worked as an intern in the press office of fashion label Chloe. Here he realised his true vocation and so, after returning to New York to complete his final year at the New School, Ford set about carving a niche for himself in the fashion business.

Ford worked first as a design assistant with sportswear designer Cathy Hardwick and then with American fashion label Perry Ellis, spending two years with each employer. Then, in 1990, he left once more for Europe where he got his first big break with Gucci, the once-prosperous leather goods and fashion brand.

Corruption and interpersonal rivalries (culminating in a contract killing) within the Gucci family had brought the Italian brand to its knees. Now under the control of an institutional investor, Gucci brought in a new creative director, Dawn Mello, with a brief to restore the label to its former glory. One of Mello's priorities was to revive Gucci's position in the women's ready-to-wear market and for that she needed fresh talent.

Mello recalls that most of those she approached 'didn't want the job'. It was a poisoned chalice and at that time, in the early 1990s, 'no one would dream of wearing Gucci'. Tom Ford was virtually unknown but Mello enticed him to Milan to become Gucci's chief womenswear designer.

From that point, Ford's career progression was rapid. From womenswear he moved quickly to menswear, then shoes and within two years he had become Gucci's design director, responsible for ready-to-wear clothes, fragrances, advertising and even store design. At one point he is reported to have been working simultaneously on no fewer than 11 product lines. Ford's success resulted not only in a revival of the brand but also contributed massively to sales. By the mid-1990s, sales at Gucci had almost doubled and on the strength of that the group went public.

In the meantime, Gucci acquired top French fashion house Yves St Laurent and, as creative director of both companies, Ford quickly made a name for himself within the industry, picking up several design awards along the way.

When he and Gucci CEO Domenico de Sole fell out with new owners PPR over artistic control of the group, Ford left to set up his own venture, taking de Sole with him as chairman of the new company. Starting with his first store, in New York, Ford established himself for the first time as a brand – furthermore, he was instantly an umbrella brand.

Drawing on his experience in product diversification at Gucci, Ford very quickly entered into a perfume collaboration with Estée Lauder and soon after that launched his own range of sunglasses. Though his products still lacked the prestige and cachet of Gucci, they were highly successful and paved the way for further development.

Pandering to consumers' desire for luxury and indulgence, Ford has cleverly mixed old-style bespoke tailoring with mass-market ready-to-wear retail efficiency, opening in-store outlets in most European, Asian and American capitals. 'We have laid the foundation necessary to become a true global luxury brand,' said Ford in 2008.

At around the time he said that, Ford made another – more surprising – announcement: he was about to unveil his first Hollywood movie. This time it was not acting that attracted him but directing. Three years previously, Ford had set up his own film company, Fade To Black, and his first film – *A Single Man*, based on the Christopher Isherwood novella of the same name – was a hit both critically and in cinemas.

Ford's move into film direction seems at first arbitrary: what could a fashion designer bring to the screen? But Ford's choice of subject, combined with his visual sensibilities, resulted in a film praised for its 'visual dazzle' and described by one critic as 'a thing of heart-stopping beauty' and by another as 'an aesthetic pleasure, like being in a designer hotel, reading a deliciously sad novel'.

The film, which stars English actor Colin Firth as a gay man mourning the death of his partner, is liberally sprinkled with Tom Ford trademarks, most notably the vintage tailoring and accessories.

A Single Man was released in 2009 and two years later Ford announced that he had a second film 'ready to go'. However, he admitted at the time, 'I would lose my mind if I just did films … Even if I cast it now it would be another 18 months before we were on set. I enjoy the speed of fashion. I love doing different things.'[4]

Brand extension is the sort of thing that luxury brands and fashion houses have always done well. Given the need to bring out at least two annual collections of their core products, these companies are unfazed by the need for

---

4   Armstrong, L. (2011) 'Tom Ford: "I'm probably the only man in England who doesn't want to dress in drag"', *The Daily Telegraph*, 7 September.

fast innovation and the power of product features. Like Gucci and Tom Ford, other luxury brands offer a wide range of complementary product categories – principally the otherwise conservative, old-school brands like Hermès, whose original core product was leather goods; Asprey, whose core products are jewellery and silverware; and Louis Vuitton, known principally for its top-of-the-range luggage. These brands now embrace a wide range of non-core products range from bespoke menswear and ladies' fashions to jewellery, gifts and watches – all of very high quality and selling at premium prices. Companies like this have usually unfurled their brand umbrellas gradually, often over many decades, while all the time keeping a close eye on their target consumers and anticipating their needs and desires.

Building an umbrella brand can take a lot of time, but if the brand is an individual who has seized the zeitgeist and enjoys global popularity, you can do it very quickly indeed. The classic example is the 'fragrance': a (usually female) celebrity fêted for her glamour, beauty and sheer ubiquity suddenly announces the launch of her own perfume. It sells well. If she's lucky, a range of cosmetics will follow; maybe a collection of shoes or clothes. Here, though, there is considerable risk involved. Building a brand around a popular entertainer, designer or media personality – what could loosely be described as a 'star' – requires that individual to remain popular, relevant and successful.

When the personality at the heart of a brand is the core product itself, the risk of brand failure is enormous. People are fickle, fallible and unpredictable – and that is as true of a brand personality as it is of the brand's consumers. What happens when your star fades? What if your brand personality starts to misbehave and attracts the wrong kind of publicity. We see this all the time when a brand seeks to promote itself by sponsoring a celebrity or paying a celebrity to endorse its product. The minute the celebrity is seen drunk in public, is caught shoplifting, is accused of beating his wife, makes an unguarded comment on a chat-show – that's when the brand pulls the plug and beats a hasty retreat. Sponsoring organisations can distance themselves if they act quickly enough, but brands built entirely around the flawed personality are usually doomed at this point.

The lesson here is that you must stay close to your customer – and that's not easy if your brand revolves around a personality who is suddenly and unceremoniously abandoned by

'Today's marketing demands a global execution capability that is much closer to consumers and is much more flexible.'

the consumer: you can't stay close to a customer who doesn't want to know you. Today's marketing demands a global execution capability that is much closer to consumers and is much more flexible. This calls for a new marketing approach that acknowledges the value of each element of the core brand and line extensions and takes into account the value of each activity not just as a stand-alone component of the brand but as a contributor to the brand as a whole. There may, for example, be activities that don't hold up as freestanding businesses but make financial sense when you look at the totality of the brand.

This brings us back to what we call the 'Lego' strategy. From a purely consumer perspective, a modern marketing strategy has to select a broad consumer proposition that provides numerous options, multiple touch-points for the product, that consumers can put together – like Lego blocks – as they see fit. This creates a highly individual end result in which the consumer is as much a part of the creation as the manufacturer. Having a single way of constructing a specific end product (end benefit) would kill the model stone dead. Construction must be left to consumers; marketers just provide the building blocks.

Giving up control of how consumers perceive and value marketing elements is highly challenging for both manufacturers and advertising agencies, who have been brought up to develop all aspects of the brand model for the consumer, limiting surprises and making the process repeatable. But we know that modern consumers are too well educated and too well connected for those old, simple, safe ways to work any longer.

So how does modern marketing create multiple touch-points to reach the largest number of consumers? The energy drink Red Bull sells in modest-sized cans for a relatively high price. Both can and product have remained unchanged for at least 25 years, but during this time, sales of Red Bull have soared and the product has acquired iconic status, and this has been achieved through a 'Lego' marketing strategy.

Red Bull's marketing platform is highly diversified and the smallest part is advertising. The company maintains a presence in a wide variety of arenas that appeal to a very wide range of consumers, while using a minimum of product imagery. Red Bull sponsors pop concerts, Formula 1 racing, numerous sports events, and extreme sports like climbing, adventure skiing and bungee jumping. It partnered the Austrian sky-diver Felix Baumgartner in his record-breaking freefall from the edge of space – a height of 38 km – in October 2012. It also owns football teams in Europe. All of these activities appeal to its main target audience of young men. While the drink is on general sale in stores, it is only made available in selected top bars around the world. The ubiquitous red bulls of its logo are not used in its television adverts; conversely, the cartoon character used in the TV ads is never used elsewhere.

Nobody summarises all this. There is no 'red thread' running through Red Bull's marketing. These are all Lego bricks, creating numerous potential touch points with the product; all have very different executions; and to a great extent, Red Bull has no control over them – particularly the sports activities. The innovation here is in the marketing mix, which creates multiple possible entry points to the product. Nobody puts it together except the individual consumer.

To end on a word of caution – some economists, notably in the US, are claiming that innovations are beginning to falter. They point out that while both the first industrial revolution (steam and railways) and the second (electricity, combustion engines, indoor sanitation, communications, entertainment, chemicals, petroleum) brought with them innovations with long-lasting effects on growth, the third industrial revolution (computers, the web, mobile telephony) seems to have generated less fundamental growth effects.[5]

This line of argument seems to point towards the ever-increasing challenge of achieving effective innovation, particularly since such innovations may have shorter and shorter effects. Of course, this may not be an argument against innovation, as such, but it does serve to show that innovations are becoming more difficult and more expensive to pull off. Yet as we have seen with Apple, a multiple and incremental approach to innovation can have unexpected and cumulative effects. Bridging the innovation gap for the FMCG means finding a way to shake off traditional methods and embrace the new, but as we shall see in the next two chapters, there are a number of barriers to overcome if such companies are to evolve into FICGs. Any innovation-led strategy is much more margin- and value-generated than a price-led activity.

---

5   Gordon, R. (2012) 'Is US Growth Over? Faltering Innovations Confront the Six Headwinds', working paper 18315, National Bureau of Economic Research, Cambridge MA.

Chapter 4

External Barriers to Innovation

Maintaining Innovative Momentum

Not all externalities hinder innovation; some actually drive it. The innovation culture at Adidas, one of the world's biggest sportswear brands, is driven by a cycle of big international sporting events such as the World Cup, the Olympic Games and myriad big annual fixtures, and the entire organisation is geared to getting the right products delivered to the customer in the right way at the right time.

Every year the company has to produce several new lines of customised products – shoes, balls, clothing and so on – ready and in its stores six weeks before the event. In fact Adidas manages a range of more than 27,000 stock keeping units (SKUs), all of which have to be updated. This is a huge organisational challenge in terms of logistics, manufacturing, recruitment and sales. Most of the primary supply chain is bought in, that is, only five per cent of the items produced come from Adidas-owned factories. This imposes even more pressure to co-ordinate the longer value chain, events and cycle plan.

One way in which Adidas copes with the stock implications of its huge range of SKUs is the electronic fitting concept it uses in its stores. Here you identify the shoe you want from a range of models on display, your foot is measured, your order sent to a manufacturing centre in China and your bespoke shoes sent to you by post. No customer need ever be told, 'I'm sorry, we don't have it in your size'. There is a premium for this service but not a large one because the store gains in other ways. It cuts down its inventory – a potential stocking nightmare when the number of lines is considered – and fewer members of staff are needed.

It's good to have innovation planning cycles driven by external events; they give focus and force Adidas to be fast and maintain a sense of urgency. It is also good to have a close rival to challenge you for first place and keep on your toes. For the last few years, the market lead has been disputed between Nike and Adidas. Sometimes they run neck and neck; in 2009 Adidas was ahead, but by 2012 Nike had taken the lead. Being the underdog can be very positive for a company in this situation; becoming top dog makes life more difficult because without that elusive goal ahead of you, you can lose direction, so this type of competitive market works for both companies.

How can FMCGs generate this kind of agility, maintain this momentum and shift to becoming FICGS? There is no denying the challenge when there are significant external and internal barriers to change. Two major external barriers are price pressure, from competition and from shareholders, and control of the supply chain.

> 'Some of the greatest obstacles to fast innovation faced by every big company are actually part of their culture and heritage.'

Unlike the successful companies that have flourished during the technological revolution of the past decade, the old blue-chip corporations were built to cope with the business challenges of the previous century, responding with strategies such as economy of scale-based manufacturing. Thus some of the greatest obstacles to fast innovation faced by every big company are actually part of their culture and heritage. They are built into their corporate attitudes and have become part of their structure and processes as strategies have been modified and optimised and grown over the years to be fit for a global marketplace. Most of these global companies emerged from strong success in big home markets, which became their blueprint for international expansion. Typically big US, German, Swiss or Japanese companies, these companies exported not only their products but also their management structures and philosophies, among them the Toyota Way and Motorola's Six Sigma. Added to this were local acquisitions that were used as springboards to new market entries. To be able to manage their multiple locations, these companies built management structures that could cover all these different regions and for the most part the original home market was not only the location of their global headquarters but became the model for all new activities, based on the assumption that 'if it works here it'll work everywhere'.

The globalisation of older companies has led to economies in manufacturing with the outsourcing of key services to low-wage geographical locations. It has also encouraged these companies to use their size and international know-how to adopt worldwide procurement policies, thereby gaining huge cost advantages over their smaller competitors.

The emergence of fast internet communications enabling the instant transfer of vast amounts of information, combined with this unprecedented freedom to buy or make a product almost anywhere in the world, has laid the foundation for massive improvements in efficiency.

This has proved so attractive that a lot of corporate energy has been devoted to productivity programmes generating hundreds of millions in savings. Consultancy firms have swarmed in and out of these global organisations bringing ever more sophisticated ways of optimising the efficiency of the operation. But these measures are often a response to the pressure to generate fast returns, with the result that the client ends up with innovation cycles running slower than their cost optimisation cycles: production becomes cheaper but the value of the offering falls even faster.

Driving down costs has its limits, of course, and any company intent on reducing its cost base must ask how far it can go before the cost reductions stop helping the business and start hurting it. A particularly good example of this is the airline industry, where for the past 20 years competition has been mainly on cost. The only way for the big airlines to compete against the new low-cost operators has been to pare everything down, with a corresponding reduction in staff and in the level of service. This has had the effect of focusing everybody on the lowest common denominator in passenger experience with the loss of all differentiation on other grounds.

> *'Any company intent on reducing its cost base must ask how far it can go before the cost reductions stop helping the business and start hurting it.'*

In the early 1990s, if you were lucky enough to be a Concorde customer, you would arrive at Heathrow Airport and go to a dedicated Concorde terminal where the Concorde Lounge would offer you the finest food and drink while you waited to board your flight. From the Concorde lounge you would walk directly on to the plane, where again you would be offered fine food and wine. Three and a half hours later you arrived in New York, at a dedicated terminal, with dedicated staff for passport control, and walked straight out to your waiting limousine. Today there is, of course, no Concorde – nor is there much of the pampered luxury and attentiveness enjoyed by the jet set of old.

Now – and only partly as a result of the security precautions prompted by the terrorist atrocities of 9/11 – first-class passengers arrive at Heathrow only to be directed to the back of the first of several queues before being shepherded into a hall with insufficient seating to await information about departure gates. After a 15-minute walk to their gate the hapless travellers are again required to stand in line as they are checked once more before boarding the plane.

Concorde was withdrawn from service in 2003, for several good reasons: a drop in passenger numbers following the fatal 2000 crash in Paris (the only accident involving Concorde in nearly 30 years of service); the general decline in air travel following the 9/11 terrorist attacks; and the loss of maintenance agreements. But was there the same need to retire a level of service along with the aircraft? The only logical explanation must be that by the early 2000s the low-cost airlines had seized control of the civil aviation industry; air travel had lost its romance and the only real growth area was in the cheap-and-cheerful budget sector.

The consumer benefited from all these internal optimisations only in terms of the lower price of basic product offerings. Just as major FMCGs are obliged today to compete on pricing in developed markets, with cut-price packages, the airlines have found themselves with no option but to reduce the 'size' of their offering in order to facilitate the lower price. As we showed in Chapter 3, where we discussed the innovation gap, price competition has become the key challenge and productivity is presented as the answer to maintaining or growing margins and profits.

A global corporation has obvious size advantages and, being global, it can call upon its international human resources and exploit cost gradients throughout the world. Cheap production in one part of the world pays dividends back home where prices are high. This works on the assumption that each market has more or less the same strategies, portfolios and competition and, by-and-large, similar consumers. On this basis the company develops and tests new concepts that, if successful, become global norms. This assumes a full alignment of markets and corporate headquarters, taking no account of vested interests in local markets, large manufacturing or large, centralised R&D.

This suits the development of future leadership, which can be sourced from an international talent pool, assuming consistent development across the organisation. A further advantage is that you can give your top talent a lot of international exposure, which is invaluable for growing high flyers. In this way they begin to develop a sense of connectivity with the consumer and an understanding of marketing, innovation and communication.

However, a lot of these advantages are sacrificed if the strategy is allowed to become regionalised. While major savings come from global programmes in all areas of the marketing disciplines, including distribution, brand management, market research and so on, regional and global centres then take up most of the developments and decision making. This distances the company from the consumer. All consumers are 'local' consumers; it's difficult to talk about the 'global' consumer.

Another price pressure comes from shareholders, seeking better dividends and return on assets. Those two great rivals, Coca-Cola and PepsiCo, offer the ideal illustration of this. In the 1990s, when both corporations were

> 'All consumers are "local" consumers; it's difficult to talk about the "global" consumer.'

the darlings of Wall Street, they sold most of their local manufacturing assets – principally, bottling plants and distribution facilities – to independent bottlers. The companies themselves were basically left with the concentrated syrup, which they supplied to a number of territorially exclusive bottlers throughout the world who held a franchise. The bottlers mixed the concentrate with sweeteners and water and produced the finished product in bottles or cans that were sold and distributed in local markets.

While this initially had an extraordinary effect on margins and returns on net assets, it also distanced the marketing departments from the consumer and cut the link that had previously enabled the company to understand local markets. It also hindered the companies' ability to innovate and expand brand programmes because it gave the regional bottlers too strong an influence over major activities.

Over the past few years, both companies have started to buy back some of the key bottlers to regain more market control and to sharpen their direct understanding of local consumers. Certainly efficiencies were starting to have a negative impact on effectiveness in regional markets. Not surprisingly, this buy-back is costing both companies a lot more money than they sold them for. But they have no choice; since they surrendered control to the bottlers, those franchisees in the biggest markets have taken charge and are not using what the company headquarters develops.

Because Coca-Cola and Pepsi do not, or cannot, innovate products quickly, they have to use other methods, such as promotions, to drive sales. This is a problem for them if the bottlers refuse to adopt the promotions they want. There's nothing the manufacturers can do if, for example, the local franchisee does not want the expense of tooling up to print special labels or designs directly onto cans. Moreover, with so much power in the hands of the bottlers, these major global companies can be surprisingly vulnerable.

In November 2012, PepsiCo Inc's partnership with a local bottling and distribution company, Serm Suk pcl, in Thailand expired. The very next day Serm Suk launched its own soft drink – Est, described as being 'much sweeter and more peppery' than Pepsi or Coke – and within two months Pepsi had virtually disappeared from stores, restaurants and vending machines throughout Thailand. The break up with the bottler meant that Pepsi no longer had access to Serm Suk's extensive distribution network and could no longer reach the market for the biggest consumers of soft drinks in Southeast Asia. Consumers reported almost immediately that it was nearly impossible to find a bottle of Pepsi in the country and analysts were predicting that Est would soon become the second biggest soft drink in Thailand, after Coke, pushing Pepsi into a low third place.[1]

So while outsourcing expensive operations in cheaper territories brings immediate cost benefits, the price in terms of losing contact with the consumer can be high. The opposite course of action, to bring everything in-house, can be very risky and is expensive. You cannot oblige part of your own company to sign a contract that gives head office the right to renege on a commitment in the event that demand unexpectedly takes a nose-dive – but you can with a small third-party supplier.

Despite the expense, from a marketing point of view, owning your entire supply chain has huge benefits. This might seem counterintuitive in terms of cost structure but it can bring a real competitive advantage, whereas outsourcing can be another external barrier to innovation.

'From a marketing point of view, owning your entire supply chain has huge benefits.'

FMCG companies have supply chain challenges because they don't have their own shops or outlets. There are often product challenges as well – food, for example, has a short shelf life. Companies whose distribution and retailing are vertically integrated can keep in touch with the consumer and can innovate quickly in order to keep the consumer interested. The classic example of how to do this is provided by Apple. The company has a strategic advantage that cannot be easily replicated because it stores its own inventory and

---

1   Lefevre, A.S. (2013) 'Pepsi suddenly scarce in Thailand after bottler break-up', *Reuters*, 22 February.

owns its own retail stores. This allows Apple to keep very close to its customers and innovate rapidly and efficiently, responding to customer feedback both before and after new innovations are launched. It is impossible for traditional companies to compete against the Apple supply chain because Apple lives by the golden rule that if you are making innovations that lead to change, you have to control the supply chain and be willing to write off investments fast. With this level of supply chain control, Apple's marketing can keep buyers at fever pitch.

With the launch of the iPod MP3 player, Apple created something almost unique: a small, beautifully designed, user-friendly and highly practical piece of personal gadgetry that everybody wanted. You could forget Sony's venerable Walkman – and indeed, everybody promptly did.

With the iPod, Apple discovered its real talent: the ability to appeal as much to consumers' emotional desires as to their practical ones. Apple's phenomenal success post-iPod is largely down to its uncanny ability not only to create things that work brilliantly, but also things that people want to possess for their own sake. People react to Apple products in the way they do to jewellery.

That Apple could create stunning designs in which to encapsulate their spectacular software programmes was already well known. As far back as 1998 the original iMacG3 made existing desktop computers, with their clunky beige plastic enclosures and separate screen and processing unit, seem instantly old-fashioned. The G3 was rounded and tactile and combined screen and processor in one brightly coloured translucent plastic casing.

With the advent of the iPod range, then the iPhone and latterly the iPad, Apple has continued building on the cachet and desirability of its products. They are all market leaders; each one is the benchmark against which rival products are measured and, most of the time, the rivals fail to measure up. It's not just that Apple products out-perform the competition, and it's not just because they stimulate that 'I-must-have-one' nerve in the customer's brain: it's a combination of both.

'Apple wraps great ideas inside great ideas,' says one online Apple fan. And that sums up the secret of Apple's success. The whole Apple experience is about promise, delivery and reward. Consumers are deliberately teased and excited, and at every stage they are both rewarded and teased again to ensure they remain in a perpetual state of eager anticipation. Being an Apple customer is like being promised a present and, as soon as the present has been unwrapped, wanting the next present as well.

This applies equally to the way Apple designs, manufactures and packages its products as well as to the way it markets, distributes and sells them. 'Apple's OS X operating system is the present waiting inside its sleek, beautiful hardware; the hardware is the present, artfully unveiled from inside the gorgeous box; the box is the present, waiting for your sticky little hands inside its museum-like Apple stores,' says professional product manager and consumer research specialist Alain Breillat. 'And the bow tying it all together? Jobs's dramatic keynote speeches, where the Christmas morning fervour is fanned on a grand stage by one of the business world's most capable hype men.'[2]

Of course, Jobs is sadly no longer with us, but his legacy lives on. Apple continues to crank up the media, through which it stimulates the customer to a condition of near-religious zeal, leading to those carefully stage-managed official launches in New York, London, Tokyo and other capitals where gadget geeks who have been camping on the sidewalk for the previous 36 hours get to race inside the Apple Store on launch day, high-fiving with the evangelical store staff before handing over however much Apple thinks it can charge to get hold of the latest device.

The entire Apple schtick seems very cleverly researched as well as seamlessly executed, and yet Steve Jobs famously insisted, 'We do no market research.' Jobs was certainly a highly talented marketer, but he never paid much attention to the notion of 'target markets', and had no time for the musings of focus groups. What Jobs and his team relied upon was their own instinctive feel for the market – a very imprecise method and certainly not one that can be readily learned.

Jobs had both an understanding of where electronic media, computing and communications were heading and a finger on the pulse of popular culture. He discovered very early that what he thought was cool was also considered cool by a very large proportion of the world's population. That is a gift granted to very few people.

Jobs explained it thus:

> It's not about pop culture, and it's not about fooling people, and it's not about convincing people that they want something they don't. We figure out what we want. And I think we're pretty good at having the

---

2   Breillat, A. 'You Can't Innovate Like Apple', www.pragmaticmarketing.com, accessed 19 February 2014.

right discipline to think through whether a lot of other people are going to want it, too. That's what we get paid to do. So you can't go out and ask people, you know, 'What's the next big thing?' There's a great quote by Henry Ford, right? He said, 'If I'd have asked my customers what they wanted, they would have told me 'a faster horse'.

Both Ford and Jobs had vision, in both cases, almost to the point of second sight. But companies that want to emulate Apple's ability to connect with consumers and develop products that will inspire and excite their customers cannot rely on Jobs' uncanny ability to think the right thoughts. In the absence of a CEO gifted with insight comparable to Jobs', the best they can do is study their market in such detail that they become adept at anticipating its needs and desires.

'The point is not to go ask your customers what they want. If you ask that question in the formative stages, then you're doing it wrong. The point is to immerse yourself in their environment and ask lots of "why" questions until you have thoroughly explored the ins and outs of their decision making, needs, wants, and problems. At that point, you should be able to break their needs and the opportunities down into a few simple statements of truth,' says Breillat.

Over-reliance on market research produces a business that paints by numbers, rather than creating its own original work. It stifles creativity and snuffs out inspiration with the result that it is very easy to launch a product that is the result of multiple compromises based on decisions made by every executive from the product manager to the marketing manager.

Although Jobs claimed not to believe in market research, there's no doubt that Apple is very much in touch with the people who buy its products and has a very good idea of not only what they want, but also of how to hook them in. A thorough understanding of those Apple thinks will be early adopters is extremely valuable during product development and Apple executives have to live the same life as their customers, immersing themselves in the music, social and technological culture of their customers.

Steve Jobs discovered that he could find out most about his market by disseminating information first, and only then re-absorbing the feedback. One of his most effective techniques was to leak early information to the media and then listen to the ensuing debate. This developed into the full-blown concept-launch, where instead of unveiling a new and fully developed product, Apple will reveal details of its proposed next generation of product.

Never foolish enough to give away the entire plot, Apple will go public with its next-generation products only when it is sure that it can bring the product to market quickly and well in advance of the competition. Crucially, though, Apple's tease is designed to stimulate enough media and industry buzz to enable the company to fine-tune its offering and make sure that when the product is finally launched it exceeds the expectations of its eager customers.

The purpose of these pre-launch presentations is of course two-fold. Besides providing a way of testing the market and making any last-minute modifications, it generates an enormous amount of publicity and whets the appetite of Apple's many eager fans. By the time the product hits the shelves, demand has usually reached fever pitch and sales are maximised.

A good example is the launch of Apple's tablet computer, the iPad, in April 2010. The device had been announced by Jobs at a much-anticipated media event in January and by the time the device became available, more than three months later, demand was raging.

Apple sold 14.8 million iPads worldwide in the first nine months of its launch, accounting for an estimated 75 per cent of tablet PC sales in 2010. Most manufacturers would be content with such widespread success, but Apple never lets the grass grow beneath its feet and by the end of the year had leaked enough information to ratchet up a new wave of hysteria over the second-generation iPad.

When the iPad 2 was announced in March 2011, the market was already eager to ditch the iPad 1 and upgrade to the new model. It went on sale the following month at the same price as the original iPad: $499 – a sleeker, slimmer and even more desirable replacement. The early adopters just had to have one. Many people who had bought their first iPad only months beforehand immediately bought the iPad 2. Sales of the remaining first generation iPad were sustained by dropping the price by $100 – a bargain, since the device was far from obsolete and was still way ahead of everything else besides its new stable mate.

At the Apple Store in New York, the iPad 2 sold out within hours of going on sale leaving a four- or five-week waiting list for online purchases. Demand was so strong that so-called 'scalpers' exploited the feeding frenzy, buying up as many devices as possible and immediately selling them on at grossly inflated prices.

According to the *New York Post*,[3] a gang of scalpers descended on Apple's Fifth Avenue store in New York on the eve of the official iPad 2 launch and paid some of the people queuing outside to help them buy up all available stock. The group then began hawking the devices at prices as high as $2,000 for a top-of-the-line iPad 2 – which retailed at $829. On eBay, one scammer managed to hike the price of a single iPad 2 to an eye-watering $13,500.

Jobs knew exactly how the market would react to his second-generation iPad, and he knew that the hysteria which greeted it was about more than the new model's extra memory, extra camera and slimmer dimensions. 'It's in Apple's DNA that technology alone is not enough,' he said during the iPad 2's pre-launch presentation in March 2011. 'It's technology married with liberal arts, married with humanities. Nowhere is that more true than in these post-PC devices.'

By January 2012 the media were again buzzing with anticipation, this time at the prospect of Apple's unveiling of the iPad 3. So deep, so earnest was the speculation that the internet had even spawned dedicated websites such as www.ipad3releasedates.net and www.ipad3latest.com,[4] which existed solely to disseminate gossip and rumours about what the next Apple product launch will bring.

'Apple is without doubt the only electronics company that is unmatched when it comes to rumours and speculations about its products. The amount of hype and frenzy that the iPad and the iPhone generate make Apple the leading company in creating such frenzy. Some of the rumours turn out to be true while others turn to be just that, rumours and this explains why Apple never comments on any speculations about its products,' reported ipad3releasedates.net, while ipad3latest.com told its visitors that: '...we are still speculating what the iPad 3 will be like. And here we have a mind-boggling rumour which is certainly out of the blue. We can expect the iPad 4, yes the iPad 4, in October of 2012.'

The runaway success of the iPad put Apple among the world's top ten brands for the first time, an elite position it shares with companies like Coca-Cola, IBM and McDonald's. In October 2012, Apple became the eighth most valuable brand in the world, according to Interbrand's annual rankings. The brand's value rose by 58 per cent to $33.5 billion (£22 billion), measured

---

3   Cartwright, L. (2011) 'iPad cads scalping buyers', *New York Post*, March 16.
4   Last accessed January 2012. These websites are now obsolete.

according to profit, future earning forecasts and the prominence of the brand. The leap was accredited to the iPad. 'Let's remember that little more than 12 months ago none of us knew what a tablet was,' Graham Hales, Chief Executive of Interbrand London, said. 'They've created demand for something none of us knew we even wanted.'[5]

Apple's supply chain looks something like this:

1.   own R&D;
2.   small own manufacture (for prototype);
3.   outsource manufacture;
4.   own warehouse stockage;
5.   distribute (by air) direct to own stores (retail).

The typical external supply chain for an FMCG looks very different:

1.   manufacture (own factory); ship to
2.   warehouse (Dubai)
3.   Dubai; distribute (by ship) to
4.   wholesalers; distribute (by land) to
5.   retailers.

Stock is required at every stage in this process, which can easily take six months and is obviously very tricky with perishable goods (for example, food, cigarettes).

These long and complex traditional supply chains – with their global reach, their layers of regional and local wholesalers and distributors and with their centrally organised retail chains – make a fast innovation cycle impossible. Most global companies need to establish highly complex roll-out schedules for their innovation pipeline, particular if they are introducing a replacement product rather than a new addition to the market. Making a global announcement, as Apple does, is impossible because the FMCG always needs to sell the old model in some countries. However, in an age where consumer communication is instant and global, these roll-outs become more and more difficult unless the price of the old model is lowered significantly.

---

5   Clark, A. (2011) 'Rise of the Apple iPad puts Apple within touching distance of the biggest brands', *The Times*, 5 October.

The cost of rapid updates also hits machine depreciation and learning curves on the making and selling side. About a year after the introduction of a new product, manufacturers have normally learned how to make it significantly more cheaply than during the launch phase. So the profits in years two and three normally offset all development costs, which makes it very attractive to maintain an unchanged product longer-term on the market. But that is how you end up in the innovation gap. It is hardly surprising that supply chain management has become a major innovation challenge for big global FMCGs.

The Real Shop Experience

Owning its own outlets is critical for Apple's strategy, as it is for companies in very different product areas, like IKEA, Zara, Starbucks and many luxury brands. These companies all need to protect and control the brand and they all own their supply chain right down to the retail level – that is, they have their own shops and not franchises – to speed up innovation and avoid the 'old inventory' effect.

One company that has perfected this process is Nestlé – one of the world's largest food companies – with its Nespresso brand. Nespresso[6] was launched in the mid-1980s as an innovative new way of brewing fresh coffee. It essentially comprised a special machine into which the user feeds one-shot capsules of real roasted and ground coffee to produce an instant cup of real café-style coffee. There was nothing else like it on the market and Nestlé was confident of success – after all, it already controlled 30 per cent of the global market for instant coffee with its famous Nescafé brand.

Nevertheless Nespresso marked a significant departure for the company since, despite its dominance of the instant coffee market, Nestlé had no significant share of the market for fresh roast-and-ground (R&G) coffee, which made up about 70 per cent of total world coffee consumption. There was a lot to play for.

R&G is what most people think of as 'real' coffee. It's what they drink in cafés, bars and restaurants and it is considered a superior product to instant granules

---

6   The following sources have been invaluable for this section: Felicias, L. (ed) (2011) *Trend-Marke Nespresso: Der Schweizer Kapsel-Boom*, FastBook Publishing; Kashani, K. and Miller, J. (2003) 'Innovation and Renovation: the Nespresso Story' (case study), IMD–5–0543, December; Lefebvre, D. (2010) *Nestlé Nespresso: Enabling the Growth of the World's Leading Coffee Producer*, Lockwood Trade Journal Co., Inc.

or powder. The Nespresso concept was therefore aimed at the top end of the coffee market. The technology that became Nespresso was invented in the mid-1970s but it was another 10 years until the concept was brought to market. By the mid- to late-1980s, premium coffee was beginning to enjoy a surge in popularity with chains like Starbucks and Costa selling greater and more exotic varieties of coffee and stimulating a renewed interest in what soon became known as 'gourmet coffee'. As 'real' coffee became fashionable again, instant coffees like Nescafé started to fall out of favour and the market began to stagnate.

Activity at the gourmet end of the market increased dramatically as the appeal of R&G coffee spread. Before long, people in the drinks industry were talking about coffee varieties and roasting processes as they would about fine wines and spirits. Some strains of coffee bean were even referred to as 'grand cru'. Nestlé quickly realised that there was huge growth potential at the luxury end of the market. Its Nespresso concept was an idea whose time had finally come.

Nespresso was initially viewed by Nestlé's Food Service division as a way into the restaurant trade. The machine and its one-shot capsules were expensive, however, and they offered restaurants nothing they could not get with a traditional espresso machine. Early trials in the restaurant sector ended in failure. But one sector that did seem to have significant potential was the office or workplace market. The self-contained capsules seemed ideal for individuals who wanted to help themselves to a really good cup of coffee whenever they felt like one; and as the machine and capsules would probably be subsidised by the employer, the high cost of each individual portion was less of an issue.

In deciding to pursue the Nespresso idea, Nestlé knew it was departing from its normal mode of operation. Nespresso wasn't just a product, like coffee powder, breakfast cereal or chocolate: it was a system of which the comestible was just one component. Nestlé had never made machines before.

In 1986, realising that this project would need a fresh approach, Nestlé set up a new, semi-autonomous, company – Nestlé Coffee Specialties (NCS) – across the road from its Lausanne headquarters to develop the Nespresso concept. This also solved a secondary problem. Nestlé represented the antithesis of luxury or gourmet products: its name was synonymous with the everyday products – cereals, instant food, baby food and pet food – in which it specialised. It wouldn't hurt if, early on, Nespresso put a bit of distance between itself and its parent company.

Machines were designed to NCS's specification by a Swiss industrial design consultancy and manufacture was licensed to another Swiss firm, Turmix. Sobal, a Swiss distributor of domestic appliances that was already active in the office coffee-machine business, was brought on board to market the Nespresso system, which included both machine and capsule.

With the Nespresso system ready for market, NCS launched it first in Italy – the world's largest espresso-drinking nation – and in its native Switzerland. Shortly thereafter the company launched Nespresso in Japan, then the world's fastest-growing coffee market. In all three markets, NCS focused exclusively on the office sector where it felt the premium price of the product would be more readily accepted.

Sales were very slow in all three markets, however, and by the end of 1987 only half of the machines already made had been sold. Problems with machine reliability dogged sales and soured relationships with new customers. NCS had missed all its targets and Nestlé was considering pulling the plug.

Camillo Pagano, then Senior Executive Vice-President for several of Nestlé's worldwide product divisions nevertheless believed in the intrinsic value of the Nespresso concept and, in an attempt to breathe new life into the venture, he head-hunted Yannick Lang, a 33-year-old, Swiss-born, US-educated former executive with tobacco giant Philip Morris. 'We needed an entrepreneur to take this further,' commented Pagano, 'and not act like a Nestlé executive'. Lang had made his name by catapulting the Marlboro clothing line from about $30 million to over $150 million in just a few years.

Lang joined NCS in 1989 and started examining the marketing philosophy behind the Nespresso concept. Who was most likely to want this expensive but very high-quality product? Employers? Probably not. Who were the drinkers of gourmet coffee? Who was spending vast amounts in places like Starbucks? Clearly, it was the wealthy middle class – for the most part sophisticated city-dwellers who knew and cared about good food and drink and who appreciated quality and style. In other words, affluent private households.

Lang was given the go-ahead to explore the private domestic market, targeting the well-educated middle classes, but only in Switzerland. And he was given an ultimatum: to triple sales volumes within the year – or Nestlé would close the business down.

Despite Lang's marketing hunch, the research didn't support the idea of a household market. In-store trial promotions with upmarket department stores failed to stimulate much interest and sales remained slow. But the Nespresso team remained convinced that their product would work. After all, they reasoned, other technologies like fax machines and mobile phones had failed in early tests.

Lang succeeded in avoiding closure of the business only by massaging his end-of-year figures to give the best possible interpretation. He remained convinced that the utilitarian office market was a dead-end and that the future lay with the private customers, many of whom already owned their own espresso machines.

The obvious route to this market was to sell the machines through specialist distributors and major retailers and to sell the capsules through supermarkets. But Lang resisted this. Why give away all the profits to these intermediaries? And supermarkets were a slow route to the end user: the capsules had a short shelf life and would be halfway to their use-by dates by the time they appeared on the supermarket shelves.

Another problem persisted: reliability. The Nespresso machines were complex and technical problems were still an issue. Lang decided that after-sales service was a key to keeping customers on board and buying their capsules. The best way to stay in touch with your end users is to sell to them direct, he realised. And so the Nespresso Club was born.

The Nespresso Club offered consumers a responsive service. When they bought their machine they automatically became members of the Club and could order their capsules direct from NCS at any time of the day or night via a dedicated telephone, fax and eventually internet service. Delivery was guaranteed within two working days and personalised advice from trained technicians was always available at the end of the line.

This was the sort of blue-sky thinking that Pagano had wanted. Nestlé had never attempted direct sales and marketing before but this looked like it could work. It did. In its first year (1990) the Nespresso Club attracted 2,700 members and had exceeded its sales target. Success led to success and the concept was rolled out across the whole of Europe over the following six years.

All the while, Lang remained alert to other marketing opportunities. He cut deals with Cathay Pacific, BA and SwissAir to serve Nespresso on their long-haul flights. He got endorsements from top European restaurateurs. And he invested heavily in training for sales and marketing staff.

And yet most of the marketing was through word of mouth. The Club saw to that; it was exclusive, it had cachet, it was aspirational. NCS hardly bothered at all with advertising, as Rupert Gasser, Nestlé's executive vice president in charge of technical, production, environment and R&D, commented: 'We don't need mass media or television. We're targeting the crème de la crème. We need simpler means, unconventional ways of reaching new consumers'.[7]

Nespresso broke even in 1995 and soon afterwards became the fastest-growing business in the Nestlé stable. By 1997 there were 220,000 members – an increase equivalent to 30 per cent year on year – and the system had won numerous plaudits from various influential bodies, including an enthusiastic endorsement from the International Institute of Coffee Tasters.

The then Nestlé CEO Peter Brabeck (1998–2009) hailed Nespresso as an object lesson in how to innovate and praised the decision to set NCS up as a semi-autonomous entity. 'You can't impose change from the top,' he said. 'You can only create an environment that stimulates change.' And he added, 'We don't want to advance the careers of those who have never made a mistake, because they've never done anything except apply the rules.'[8] It was important, he said, to identify, foster and mentor people who have shown a willingness to stick their necks out.

Lang's success with Nespresso did not go unnoticed and in 1997 he was lured away from Nestlé by another food company. His replacement was an in-house appointment: Willem Pronk, a 44-year-old executive and a Nestlé man through and through. Although no maverick, Pronk had a reputation for taking risks and making things happen, having achieved a 200 per cent increase in Nescafé sales in the Netherlands. He would need all his skills to achieve what his employer demanded at Nespresso: namely to take the business from its present SFr150 million turnover to SFr1 billion in the next ten years.

---

7   Kashani, K. and Miller, J. (2003) 'Innovation and Renovation: The Nespresso Story' (case study), IMD–5–0543, December.
8   Kashani, K. and Miller, J. (2003) 'Innovation and Renovation: The Nespresso Story' (case study), IMD–5–0543, December.

Pronk built on Lang's principle of remaining close to the end user. He used computer modelling to map customers' buying habits so that his sales team could intervene when something went awry – for example, if they failed to place an order within a predicted timescale.

He introduced free machine servicing, with a complimentary replacement when a customer's machine needed repair. Such measures were designed to create customer intimacy and build long-term customer loyalty.

Nespresso had created and dominated a new gourmet coffee market sector: portion coffee. But while it had the market almost to itself, it was still a small part of a much bigger picture. Research commissioned by Pronk revealed only five per cent awareness in target markets and less than one per cent penetration of domestic households. Very few coffee drinkers actually knew about Nespresso.

Pronk wanted to expand the appeal of Nespresso and to do so he had to raise public awareness of the product drastically. Again, advertising was ruled out – Pagano was 'worried about the mass-market mentality entering the picture'.[9] Nespresso, after all, was a luxury brand and exclusivity was part of its appeal.

Product placement was considered, with machines and capsules being gifted to influential people such as politicians and top journalists. Many machines were also given away as demonstrators to leading retailers. In Belgium alone, NCS gave away 2,100 Nespresso machines in 1998. But the results were disappointing.

Although this exercise succeeded in recruiting new members of the Nespresso Club, it quickly emerged that more than half of all new members never called the Club for top-up capsules. After a year, only 26 per cent were still active. Pronk suddenly realised the mistake: they'd been over-promoting to people who actually didn't drink much coffee: 'If we promote the machines too much, we'll succeed in getting people to buy the machines but not the complete concept,' he observed.[10]

There was no escaping the fact that Nespresso was the most expensive way of making coffee: five times the cost per cup of filter coffee and three times as much as regular espresso. Going down-market was not an option. Nespresso was aimed at the top 10 per cent of households who, if they could

---

9   Kashani, K. and Miller, J. (2003) 'Innovation and Renovation: The Nespresso Story' (case study), IMD–5–0543, December.

10 Kashani, K. and Miller, J. (2003) 'Innovation and Renovation: The Nespresso Story' (case study), IMD–5–0543, December.

afford the machine, could certainly afford the capsules. Another sub-segment of this target group also began to be significant: the growing number of single-person households as a result of increased divorce rates in Europe. Nespresso represents an overall cost advantage in the single household, where someone will probably drink only one or two cups a day – much cheaper than buying the drink from a Starbucks, Costa or similar.

Swiss retailers were keen to persuade NCS to let them sell the capsules, but again Pronk resisted. Not only would that be giving the profit to other people, it would also mean losing the invaluable consumer knowledge obtained through the Club.

On the other hand, the retail idea was not such a bad one, Pronk decided. Just as the Nespresso Club had been a step into the unknown territory of direct sales, NCS was soon preparing to make another bold move, this time into retail. Opening a chain of exclusive 'coffee boutiques' in select locations would raise awareness significantly without taking the brand down-market. So, with a strict investment budget of SFr250,000 per outlet, NCS opened its first boutiques in carefully chosen European cities.

The strategy worked. Wealthy shoppers were lured in and sales grew accordingly. More than 13 years after its launch, Nespresso was finally performing reliably and sales were growing, though they still fell far short of Brabeck's SFr1 billion target.

Nespresso had created the portion-coffee sector and still controlled 90 per cent of the market. But there were now several rivals, keen to grab a piece of the action, claiming the remaining 10 per cent. Fortunately for NCS, most of these competitors were still targeting the office market and their products were more down-market and of lower quality. Pronk knew there was no room for complacency – after all, the Nespresso patents would soon expire – but he was well ahead of the crowd. He had superior technology and of course the all-important Nespresso Club.

It would take any newcomer hoping to grab more market share a good four years to establish a foothold in any national market. And they would need a minimum of 15,000 installed machines to break even.

For most manufacturers, going into retail in a sophisticated market environment with huge and very efficient third-party networks of wholesalers, distributors and modern retail chains, does not make much sense. It imposes a

massive burden on profitability because of the enormous investment required
in stores, warehouses and transport. It also adds considerably to employment
costs – something all major corporations try to reduce.

So why do it?

As the Nespresso example illustrates, the answer is control. If you own
the retail outlet you control not only what products are displayed and how,
but you also control the customer interface. This gives you that invaluable
on-the-spot, real-time feedback information that informs your marketing
and R&D activities and allows you to deliver what people want, when they
want it. But there are different ways to achieve a similar end result through
store ownership, and while Nespresso made their stores all about the coffee,
its great high-street rival Starbucks
made them all about the experience,
which gives Starbucks the kind of
multiple touch-points that amplify
the customer relationship.

> 'If you own the retail outlet you control not
> only what products are displayed and how,
> but you also control the customer interface.'

Starbucks also started out as a coffee retailer, though of a very different
kind from Nespresso. It began life not as a spin-off from a global food giant,
but as a small independent company selling a range of roasted and green coffee
beans and loose tea to a small but discerning clientele in its native Seattle. Of
course today it is itself a giant global brand but its success owes less to the
reputation of its coffee (good though no doubt it is) and more to its image as
the provider of an attractive, healthy and sophisticated metropolitan lifestyle.

The company's raison d'être is neatly summed up by marketing guru Scott
Bedbury, who, as Senior Vice President of Marketing at Starbucks in the mid-
1990s, spearheaded a major re-launch of the brand:

> Starbucks' role is to provide uplifting moments to people every day. I
> didn't say coffee. If you go beyond coffee, you can get to music, you can
> get to literature, you can get to a number of different areas ... Just like
> when you drop a rock in a pond there will be ripples that come outside
> that core ... Starbucks is not just a pound of coffee but a total coffee
> experience.[11]

---

11 Joseph L. Rotman School of Management, University of Toronto, 'The Starbucks Brand',
    Rotman Case Series (no date or author name supplied).

Starbucks made the leap from regional coffee retailer to global brand under the leadership of CEO Howard Schulz. He joined the company in 1982 as Director of Marketing and it was while in Milan on a buying trip that he noticed that there was a coffee shop on every street that not only served excellent espresso but also provided informal gathering places and met an important social need.

On his return to Seattle, Schultz tried to persuade his Starbucks colleagues to offer a café service in addition to selling the beans, tea and spices from the retail counter. A trial café proved successful, but the Starbucks owners refused to build on this early success for fear of diluting their core retail activity.

Frustrated, Schultz left Starbucks to open his own coffee house, which he called Il Giornale. Shortly thereafter, the owners of Starbucks bought the Californian coffee specialist Peets (which had been the inspiration behind the original Starbucks retail business) and sold Starbucks to Schultz. He promptly dropped the Il Giornale name in preference to the well-known Starbucks brand and embarked upon his long-held ambition to roll out a national chain of high-quality coffee houses.

Schultz continued to draw inspiration from the relaxed social environment he had witnessed in the Milanese coffee houses he had visited years before. He was convinced that the same values of quality, comfort, social interaction and relaxation would work just as well in North America as in Italy.

He started to build the Starbucks chain on four guiding principles: coffee as a healthy lifestyle alternative to alcohol; the provision of a welcoming, comfortable meeting place where people could relax and interact informally; the promotion of high-quality 'gourmet' coffee as an affordable luxury; and the presentation of coffee as a fashionable consumer product and symbol of sophisticated tastes.

Since those early days, one of Schultz's most effective marketing techniques has been to add value to the coffee experience not simply by offering a wide variety of styles and recipes but also by providing his customers with information. In a move that could have easily backfired as seeming patronising or pretentious, Starbucks set about educating its customers, providing information both printed and verbal at the point of consumption. Just as people with sophisticated tastes may aspire to becoming a wine buff, so Schultz's customers were encouraged to become coffee buffs.

Ever since the emergence of the *Wiener Kaffeehaus* culture in eighteenth-century Vienna, the coffee house has enjoyed a reputation for attracting intellectuals and artists. That tradition enjoyed a renaissance in 1990s North America just as Starbucks was entering its fastest period of growth. Research carried out in the early 1990s showed that coffee drinkers were mainly educated, middle-class and well off.

Then in 1994 a new TV situation comedy, depicting the lives of six young, attractive, fashionable friends who meet regularly in a Greenwich Village coffee house called 'Central Perk' was launched on American TV. Schultz's vision of the coffee house as a desirable lifestyle signifier had finally come true. *Friends* quickly became one of the most popular sitcoms of all time, propelling its cast towards international stardom.

Starbucks' career followed the same stellar route. By 2003 the company had more than 7,500 locations worldwide and net revenues of over $4 billion. It was voted one of *Adweek*'s 'most trusted brands'.

Just as Schultz had predicted, the coffee house had replaced bars, restaurants and clubs as the principal meeting place for many urban professionals. And the Starbucks brand was all-conquering. It was built on three core elements: its coffee, its people and its stores – with quality a key ingredient of all three. Starbucks from the very outset was extremely demanding of its suppliers. It would carry out quality checks on fresh beans before shipping, on reaching the destination and on delivery to the stores, and reserved the right to refuse a consignment at any stage.

Staff members were carefully chosen and a lot of time and effort were invested in their training. Starbucks quickly earned a reputation for paying its staff more than the fast-food sector's average wage and its stock option plan (known as Bean Stock) was made open to all employees, regardless of seniority. Staff turnover is generally less than half the industry average.

Significantly, Starbucks owns every one of its outlets, preferring to retain control rather than entrust the brand image to an army of franchisees. The company places great emphasis on creating the right environment, a relaxing destination where the smell of fresh coffee mingles with a warm, comfortable and welcoming atmosphere. Mystery shoppers regularly pay each store a visit to check on the ambience and service.

Schulz's philosophy is that successful brands evolve from 'everything the company does'. The Starbucks experience therefore goes well beyond coffee, offering customers 'great people, first rate music, a comfortable and upbeat meeting place and sound advice on brewing excellent coffee at home'. Each Starbucks store, meanwhile, should be a 'third place' – 'at home you're part of the family; at work you're part of the company,' commented Schultz. Starbucks should be 'a place where you can sit back and be yourself'.[12]

Starbucks has not grown to its present dominant position without having attracted some criticism. In particular, it has been accused of using its economic might to squeeze small independents out of prime locations by operating some stores at a loss or opening multiple outlets in a selected area.

Nevertheless, Starbucks would prefer to attribute its market dominance to its core values of maintaining 'the highest standards of excellence in purchasing, roasting and delivering' its coffee; 'nurturing enthusiastically satisfied customers', 'contributing positively to the community' and 'recognizing that profitability is essential to future growth'.

Ron Kaufmann, founder of service performance consultancy UP! Your Service, comments: 'Starbucks is an extraordinary example of a company with loyal customers and vigorous global growth ... One reason is their devotion to customer service quality. Another is their fanatical commitment to cultivating customers through attractive and persistent education, which raises the customer service quality bar.'[13]

No traditional FMCG company can claim to enjoy the close contact with the consumers of their product that Starbucks enjoys. Even major retailers struggle to achieve the same levels of customer engagement. But Starbucks is an example of the modern approach to supply chain integration in which control of every stage of production from manufacture right through to direct customer interactivity is characteristic.

There are industries where such a level of supply chain integration is almost unknown, including the fashion business, which is renowned for its use of outsourcing. Indeed, many fashion labels have come under attack for what is perceived as their exploitation of low-paid, underage workers in the

---

12 Joseph L. Rotman School of Management, University of Toronto, 'The Starbucks Brand', Rotman Case Series (no date or author name supplied).
13 Kaufman, R. 'Education Makes Starbucks' Customer Service Quality Star Shine', www.upyourservice.com, accessed 18 February 2014.

developing world. But Spanish fashion company Zara has bucked that trend and made control of the entire supply chain an article of corporate faith, demonstrating that traditional methods and old habits can be disrupted. The company not only shows the massive advantage of being able to innovate quickly, but also the benefits of controlling supply all the way to the customer – and back.

Launched in the 1970s by aspiring entrepreneur Amancio Ortega Gaona, Zara is the flagship brand of Ortega's Industria de Diseño Textil (Inditex), one of the world's top fashion producers. Ortega himself is now Spain's richest man and was ranked the eighth richest in the world in 2007. As of the end of 2012, Zara had 120,000 employees worldwide, was present in 86 countries and owned 1,750 stores.

Zara's original strategy was to sell quality designer fashions at reasonable prices – a plan that had already worked well for Gap in the US and for Next in the UK.

With his knack for opening stores in top locations, Ortega quickly developed a loyal following simply by word of mouth. After Inditex went public in 1999, the Group's first annual report set out Ortega's philosophy in clear terms: 'To democratise fashion. In contrast to the idea of fashion as a privilege, we offer accessible fashion that reaches the high street, inspired by the taste, desires, and lifestyle of modern men and women.'[14]

Zara's success was built on the concept of 'fast-fashion', which relies on bringing new products from the design stage to the store as quickly as possible. This gives Zara the ability to respond instantly to developing trends; the company can hit the high street with its own versions of designs from top names in the fashion industry within a couple of weeks of the originals appearing on catwalks in Paris, Milan or New York.

In order to respond so quickly, Zara has rejected the path taken by most clothing retailers. Instead of outsourcing design and production to low-cost workshops in the developing world, the Spanish company has retained control of the entire supply chain, designing its clothes itself and having most of them made by local subcontractors.

---

14   Nash, E. (1999) 'The discreet mogul fashioning an empire', *The Independent* 27 October.

This enables Zara to get clothes from design to store up to 12 times faster than the competition. Being able to respond so quickly allows Zara to avoid high inventory costs and avoid the frequent clearance sales so common among other clothing retailers. Stores report back regularly to head office to say which lines are selling and which are not and production is adjusted to meet customer requirements. Because the clothes are nearly all made in Europe, Zara ships fewer items, in greater variety and more often than the competition, while enjoying lower shipping costs and producing only what is needed by the stores themselves.

All of Zara's clothes are finished off at the company headquarters in La Coruña, northern Spain, before being shipped out twice a week to the company's stores. The fact that it can react quickly to changing fashion trends allows Zara to remain fresh and always ahead of its main rivals.

One consequence of the regular delivery of new stock is that customers know when a new consignment is due in and will check out their local store on a regular basis to find the latest designs. Another consequence is that popular items tend to appear and disappear quickly, often within a week, thus creating the appearance of exclusivity, which enhances their appeal.

Customer loyalty is thereby reinforced and word of mouth has become an important factor in promoting the brand. Ortega discovered at a very early stage that the grapevine is a powerful sales tool and Zara became successful so quickly that advertising has almost never been necessary; word of mouth has always maintained sales.

That is not to say that Zara does not have a media profile. The company's success has ensured that many column inches are regularly devoted to its activities – and most of the publicity has been positive. Although the company is reported to spend up to 15 per cent more on labour costs than most of its rivals, the fact that its factories are mostly in Europe means that it has escaped many of the accusations of sweatshop and child-labour exploitation levelled at its rivals.

The one notable exception is a recent incident in which a Brazilian factory subcontracted to Zara was found to be employing underpaid workers from Bolivia and Peru. The firm moved quickly to address the problem, but despite some bad publicity the incident proved, if anything, the ethical foundation underlying Zara's supply chain model.

As a Spanish company, Zara can exploit the tradition of small artisan workshops that has persisted throughout the Iberian peninsula, giving it a flexible supply-base located close to the head office. This coincidence of resources has allowed Ortega to make Zara what Daniel Piette, Fashion Director of Louis Vuitton, has described as 'the most innovative and devastating retailer in the world'.[15]

The own-store model also works for manufacturers of luxury products because they can create their own ambience and control the shopping experience. This is especially important in the haute couture and designer sector of the fashion market, where ambience is part of the product and outlet ownership is crucial. The service offered and the way in which the product is presented are part of the brand message. Retail outlets can be tailored to local needs and updated instantly. Luxury labels also have their own staff, so are in control of recruitment and training.

The FMCG and the Supply Chain

The combination of internet shopping and the twenty-first century real shop experience represents a huge challenge for the old FMCGs and they have struggled to meet it.

One option pursued by many FMCGs has been to optimise supply chain costs by partnering with organised trade, but this leads to a critical loss of control, a reliance on the external supply chain and a loss of contact with the customer. Around 85 per cent of products are sold in this way via major supermarket chains; in most western European markets the top three supermarket chains control up to 60 per cent of all FMCG sales. These relationships are handled by key account managers and most FMCGs develop tailor-made products and promotions for these powerful retail outlets, including special production runs, custom sizes, tailored promotions and seasonal offers. Once the products have been manufactured they are sent to the warehouse or distributor for organised trade at which point the manufacturer loses control. With 85 per cent of all products going into organised trade, the manufacturer needs no field personnel to sell to individual stores because all purchasing is done centrally. And while this reduces the manufacturer's fixed costs, it increases their reliance on the supply chain, reducing their control over which products go where, when, and how they are displayed. The big savings in fixed costs are offset by this loss

---

15 Hume, M. (2011) 'The secrets of Zara's success', *The Daily Telegraph*, 22 June.

of control – and power shifts to trade. As we saw with Coke and Pepsi earlier, the ability to innovate is much reduced if you have to rely on an externally controlled supply chain.

However, some companies have been willing to take the risk to reinvent their supply chains, wresting control of distribution back from third parties. BAT in Canada did exactly this – and everyone thought the firm was crazy. BAT wanted to keep control of its product in stores, so had no choice but to strengthen the vertical supply chain, selling directly to retailers and delivering products. This was expensive but BAT knew it was the only way to keep control, having had direct experience of this in Russia. When the ruble crashed in 1998, hard currency prices rose by 40 per cent in Russia and if BAT had not had control at store level, it would have had no control over price rises. By retaining control in the stores, a company can support prices and not lose sales. It can also introduce new products, buying back the old if necessary.

Nowadays, analysts think managing your supply chain is an advantage, but they certainly didn't in 2000, when this initiative was launched. In fact, it took BAT marketing a good decade to convince the organisation and the analysts that it was a worthwhile route. However, BAT beat the competition because of innovations consumers appreciated. Rahul Prakash, ex-Head of Global Trade Marketing and Distribution (TM&D) and the Canadian Head of TM&D at the time, describes how BAT established competitive advantage through direct to store sales of tobacco products in Canada:

> The Canadian Tobacco market was a BAT marketer's dream. In 2000, BAT's subsidiary in Canada, Imperial Tobacco Limited Canada (ITL), had over 69 per cent share of a market that operated at one price – premium. And BAT had over 70 per cent share of the premium segment. In 2001 there was a severe excise hike and the premium segment declined from 99 per cent to 98 per cent of the total market. ITL saw no need to panic; in fact it took the opportunity to raise prices. But by 2002 the decline in premium was even steeper, to 94 per cent share of the total market. Even though these pricing moves by ITL resulted in record profits that year, ITL's market share declined to 67.7 per cent. Now there was concern … but there was worse to come. Traditionally, all the major manufacturers in Canada had followed Imperial Canada's lead in pricing. However, in 2003, in a discontinuous move, the Phillip Morris subsidiary Rothmans B&H Canada (RB&H) priced down Number 7, a brand with relatively small national share, by $1 per pack. It took some months for consumers to grasp fully the impact of this move, but once they did, ITL's portfolio of brands – DuMaurier, Players, Matinee – suddenly looked frayed. Their price–value equation started to erode. Pricing down one of the major brands was not an option BAT was prepared to contemplate since the

profit impact of any such move had high and immediate bottom-line impact – in hundreds of millions of dollars. The company ended the year disastrously as its market share tumbled to 63.4 per cent. It tried to adapt to the new reality, which refused to go away, by pricing down Peter Jackson, a strong player in Quebec province, while simultaneously instructing the field force not to push this offer too hard.

The scale of the marketing challenge became evident early on, though few in the group were willing to accept it. Marketing restrictions made consumer communication very challenging and ITL lacked the ability to deliver impact where it mattered most in the Canadian market – at points of purchase and points of consumption. What was clear and agreed, though, was that these marketing restrictions were set to intensify and tobacco was clearly becoming 'de-normalised'. Through all this RB&H continued to evolve its price positioning strategy, and in 2004 launched Canadian Classic, deceptively similar in positioning to ITL's Players, at a price point even lower than Number 7. Through 2004 and 2005 ITL's share tumbled to just over 55 per cent – a decline of more than 14 per cent in five years. Still, a 55 per cent share is sizeable and significant. The question was, could ITL leverage its market position, albeit declining, to steady its share from what appeared a terminal decline? Through 2004 and 2005 the case for direct-to-store sales (DSS) had been gaining momentum as a means of leveraging existing share, delivering marketing impact at points of purchase and points of consumption, and creating long-term competitive advantage for ITL.

This case was built upon five pillars:

1.   ITL's control over the retail trade was narrow and eroding. The growth of the cash-and-carry channel, which was in excess of 30 per cent, exacerbated the problem. ITL's ability to market effectively to the consumer was becoming more and more difficult with the passage of time.

2.   Despite the fact that ITL provided wholesalers with a major subsidy, they did not reciprocate with any significant structured 'push' for ITL's brands. Instead, they used this subsidy to cut the price to their customers of their entire basket of goods in a bid to improve their distribution competitiveness.

3.   As markets became more restricted and ITL's ability to establish a trade marketing dialogue with retailers was eroded, a direct commercial relationship offered that possibility through the introduction of commercial trading terms, which they would follow.

4.   *Within the dominant channel of retail sale (the convenience store), ITL accounted for around 40 per cent of the retailers' profitability, grounds enough for them to respond positively to efforts to extend the commercial relationship.*

5.   *This would create a competitive advantage for ITL by lifting the price of distribution for competitors in existing wholesale and cash-and-carry channels.*

However, there were several significant unanswered questions: would there be retailer buy-in? What would it cost? And what real advantage would ITL gain? How would ITL deal with existing wholesalers, some of whom were their largest customers – retailers with their own wholesale and cash-and-carry arm such as Loblaws and Sobeys? Even within the company itself there was incredulity that ITL would even contemplate such a move. Why upset the apple cart of route to market, which seemed to work well, just when the rest of the marketing strategy was already under tremendous pressure? With strong views and arguments on both sides, and an emotionally charged atmosphere whenever DSS was discussed, ITL decided to settle the matter once and for all by embarking on a project that would examine the issue in depth and recommend actions to the ITL and BAT boards.

'Project Hat Trick' was launched with consultants McKinsey with five clearly defined deliverables within specified timeframes. Each of the five stages was a 'gate' for the ITL and BAT boards to approve before transition to the next stage. These stages were:

1.   *Proof of concept, March–June 2005.*

2.   *Detailed design and planning, August–December 2005.*

3.   *Detailed implementation planning, January–August 2006.*

4.   *Approve go-live, September 2006.*

5.   *Post go-live support, October 2006–March 2007.*

A hat trick in sport is the achievement of a positive feat three times during a game, or other achievements based on threes. ITL's Project Hat Trick also had three interrelated objectives:

1.   *To deliver a world-class DSS model that ensured better distribution of ITL brands in the market.*

2.   *To use DSS as a means of introducing effective marketing at points of purchase and points of communication for their brands.*

3.   *To create a strategic change in the route-to-market model in Canada that competitors would find difficult if not impossible to follow.*

Despite early setbacks during implementation, the project delivered robustly on all three objectives. Two factors were critical to this success – the structural and implementation design of the project. For its two-year life-cycle, Project Hat Trick was led by the management board at ITL. This gave the project the attention and respect it needed within the company. More importantly, since this was a 'secret' project, conducted from a 'secret' location outside ITL offices, board-level leadership provided much-needed assurance to the 50 or so people working on it full-time during this period. Second, to ensure that management owned and adopted the outcomes from the project, 10 sub-teams were created, each led by a departmental head within the company. The sub-teams covered key accounts, trade development, trade terms, credit and finance, corporate and regulatory affairs (CORA), sales, supply chain, HR, IT and legal. Unsurprisingly, the largest sub-teams were IT, followed by supply chain.

In addition to support from McKinsey, project delivery was tracked for quality by a team of internal auditors who constituted the quality assurance (QA) team and reported independently to the ITL management board.

Early in the project it became clear that ITL did not have the required logistical expertise and knowledge to manage the DSS network structure and the product flows through it. As a result of this discovery, ITL evaluated several logistics providers and settled on Ryder Corporation as its distribution partner. The Ryder team worked seamlessly as an integral part of the ITL Hat Trick team and this relationship has stood the test of time. In other words, from its inception, the project was structured to deliver unqualified and unambiguous answers at each stage, which could be implemented flawlessly once the decision was taken to move ahead.

At the end of 2005, the BAT board approved the DSS business case, and ratified ITL's decision to move ahead with the project. Given the need for secrecy and speed, several key issues had to be addressed in implementation design. The first was how ITL could create trade terms that made a compelling case for retailers to accept DSS in a market where almost 60 per cent of sales was made to key accounts – large retailers owning multiple sales outlets. To make matters even more interesting, some of the largest retailers were vertically integrated; in other words, they sold through retail outlets, and also had large cash-and-carry operations, which would be jeopardised by ITL's proposals. ITL had to decide how it could change trade terms within the letter and spirit of the law without giving away too much prematurely and thus jeopardising its existing business relationships. This was a cornerstone of the entire business case, which assumed that ITL would claw back $60m annually from the wholesale trade.

There remained several unanswered questions for ITL. How was it going to recruit the large number of staff necessary without giving away the plot? It would need to recruit around 350 sales staff and Ryder an additional 650–700 logistics staff. Previously, very small numbers had been recruited into the ITL sales force. Also, how would the IT transformation take place? The project was heavily reliant on the success of the IT model, which included changing the customer relationship management (CRM) model from around 95 customers to over 28,000. Then there were the modifications needed to the network of warehouses, hitherto catering for a small number of wholesale customers, in order to fit the needs of an exponentially larger customer base. There was also the problem of managing accounts received from tens of thousands of small retailers – this had been simple when the customer base comprised just a handful of large wholesalers. And then there was the question of how to train and re-train the large numbers of staff involved. Finding the answers to these questions was critical to the success of the project. ITL addressed them head-on in the implementation design and pre-launch phase, so that once implementation began there would be no ambiguities about intent.

ITL's senior management team embarked on a whirlwind tour of the country to introduce the new trade terms to their key customers. The first meeting took place on a cold autumnal morning with the largest retail customer in Laval, a suburb of Montreal. There was incredulity and disbelief. Nothing like this had ever been done before in Canada. (ITL discovered later that a change of this magnitude had not been made in North America for the previous 50 years.) They knew that change was coming in ITL's route to market but none was prepared for its scale and magnitude. In essence, trade terms were designed around retailers. These were published and freely available. ITL defined a retailer as a sales outlet that sold exclusively to consumers. This meant that vertically integrated accounts that had both a wholesale and a retail operation would obtain favourable terms for their retail sales that would not be available for wholesale sales. ITL had a history of sales per retail outlet and it was impossible for the trade to manipulate numbers. Further, ITL raised invoice prices to fund the trade terms and recapture the wholesale margin. Wholesalers found that they just could not compete with ITL prices to retail. Conversely, retailers found they could not refuse ITL's offer.

In order to ensure secrecy, ITL, in its earlier communication with the trade, gave away just enough to meet its obligations but not enough to tell the full story. Similarly, to recruit the large number of fresh graduates, ITL's recruiters had visited all the major campuses in Canada, and interviewed the graduating batch of 2006. Canada is huge, and it was difficult to connect the fact that ITL was recruiting in each major university from Victoria to Newfoundland. Every candidate recruited met ITL's recruitment criteria in a record period of time. With three months to go before 'D-Day', training began in earnest. The training programme focused on building technical skills, imparting knowledge and building a can-do attitude. Detailed training programmes had been designed to accomplish this. By the time D-Day came around on 5 September, every new recruit had 'graduated' the ITL academy.

Ryder recruitment was simpler since the company was known to be a large logistics provider. However, training was more of a challenge. Not many operations had the pick-and-pack in seven warehouses that Ryder had to contend with. In addition, the team had little experience of DSS and did not quite know what to expect. Still, they did go through a timely round of training with their core staff. Even more difficult was ensuring that the IT backbone was robust. Retail orders were generated by the reps, transferred automatically to the ITL server in Montreal, transferred to the Ryder server in Atlanta, which aggregated them, and transferred back to ITL to create sequenced invoices. On the basis of this Ryder's warehouse team picked and packed the orders overnight to load onto trucks for transfer to cross-dock locations or to vans for next-day delivery. The system worked smoothly in simulated trials.

On ITL's side, IT transformation and movement to its new CRM platform – V3, an in-house global standard – went even more smoothly. In fact, once the decision to use BAT's CRM platforms had been taken, the transformation was flawless. The challenge of building a physical network to cater to the DSS operation was also complex. The design called for seven warehouses, 14 cross-dock locations, 225 vans and trucks, 200 delivery routes, 215 drivers, 120 administration staff and over 500 material handlers. At go-live all locations bar one – Calgary – were functional; given the complexity and the interrelated nature of the implementation, it was not possible to delay the entire implementation for Calgary. The challenge of ensuring that the accounts received did not get out of hand was managed with precision – ITL trade terms offered 50 cents per carton for pre-payment and virtually all customers accepted these terms. In other words, on the day goods were shipped to them customers transferred the invoice amount to the ITL account. The positive cash flow generated by this one move alone was in the millions of dollars.

Co-ordination of this complex activity was undertaken by the 'War Room', which worked round the clock. There were daily calls with each of the six regions starting at 6 am with the maritime zones and ending at 11 pm with Vancouver, BC. Every detail was tracked, however small. The ITL management board received formal weekly briefings but most board members chose to sit in on the daily conference calls with the regions and offer guidance and advice. At the end of the implementation phase *everything seemed to have gone well with the exception of the full readiness of Calgary warehouse, and even there the team was confident that it would be possible to make deliveries. 'Go-live' was 5 September 2006, by which time over 90 per cent of all retailers had signed up for DSS. ITL's best estimates for DSS sign up had been 60 per cent. Acceptance was overwhelming. Even prior to go-live, one of ITL's large key account customers, based in Western Canada, faxed orders for all their outlets across the country. Reps collected orders with no hiccups. Throughout the day on D-Day orders were routinely loaded to the ITL server. Then all hell broke loose.*

Instead of taking under a second for each order to transfer from the Ryder server back to the ITL server, it took ten seconds per order. As a result a tremendous backlog of unpicked orders built up. Retailers had paid for orders on the planned day of shipment and many did not receive goods against those payments. ITL's customer care line was jammed solid with irate customers demanding their goods. The problem was worst in Calgary. Over the next weeks, ITL and Ryder did their best to fix the IT problem that had overwhelmed their communication lines. The sales and delivery team worked overtime to fill back orders and restore normality. Over the period of a few weeks things did get back to normal, but this hitch, created by a failure in IT communication, left a bad feeling that took the sales team a long time to resolve. Nevertheless, nine months after go-live, when the project phase ended three months later than planned, the project had delivered robustly on most objectives. The move to DSS was a change of immense magnitude. The management board at BAT and the ITL board demonstrated considerable strategic and tactical leadership to guide the programme to success. The project had its desired effect, creating a strategic discontinuity in the market and giving ITL an advantage that none of the competitors could follow. It was a move that will go down in marketing folklore in Canada.

The costs of owning your own supply chain are very high and the risks considerable. It is hard to make a convincing business case for it. Are retailing and distribution your core competences? Probably not. How long will it be before you see the payout? Add a little recession to the mix and you get an idea of how hard it will be to keep both your job and the shops.

Moving from an indirect supply chain to a direct selling one will be an enormous financial adventure but also a big business and legal challenge. You will be taking over from a lot of businesses – distributors and wholesalers – something

> *'If you really believe in faster innovation cycles, a radically more flexible supply chain could be the key to their implementation and success.'*

they see as their own. What's more, you will be going against an organised supply chain where your product is just one among many and carries overheads. You will make real enemies, whom your competition will be only too happy to exploit. In reality, you can only do this with a lot of confidence in the endgame and the support of an aligned organisation. But in the end if you really believe in faster innovation cycles, a radically more flexible supply chain could be the key to their implementation and success – though not necessarily, as we will see in the next chapter.

Chapter 5

Internal Barriers to Innovation

New thoughts and new ideas typically go through three stages; first they get ridiculed, then they meet very strong resistance, finally they get accepted as truth.

R.P. Schopenhauer, 1788–1860

First they ignore you, then they laugh at you, then they fight you, then you win.

Mahatma Gandhi

'If only HP knew what HP knows, we would be three times more productive.' These words, from former CEO of Hewlett Packard, Lew Platt, will resonate with anyone who works in a large organisation. Knowledge transfer and knowledge creation are major concerns in complex organisational structures that create a lot of 'noise' above which individuals have great difficulty being heard. Many companies go out of their way to create opportunities to exploit the hidden knowledge within their organisations by improving communication and connections both within the organisation and externally, with suppliers, distributors, business partners and customers.

Enormous amounts of time and energy go into this. Project-based work involves the construction of teams that are diverse by design, bringing together people with different functional expertise and different leadership styles to maximise the innovative capacity of the team. Organisational hierarchies are flattened to accommodate eclectic creative combinations within teams; office layouts are changed to stimulate new connections between individuals; people are seconded to other departments to hot desk for periods of time. The formal and informal networking groups within the organisation are tapped – the squash players, the gym users, even the smokers. The company newsletter posts information about people's activities within and outside the organisation: what projects they are working on, their connections with the wider community, extra-curricular sporting achievements, fundraising for charity and so on. People are encouraged to drop ideas into suggestions boxes while handpicked groups are whisked away for a week's brainstorming at an out-of-town location. At some firms, people are encouraged to eat collectively in the company's subsidised cafés and mix with others. Lunches out or at their desks are frowned upon.[1]

Some of these efforts are highly effective. Oticon, the Danish hearing-aid manufacturer, transformed itself from 'a traditional hierarchical, departmental, slow-moving organisation' in the 1990s by literally pulling down the walls in its headquarters, equipping its people with movable desks, creating a 'paperless' environment and ensuring everyone in the organisation undertook several functions, as well as operating within their own specialism. 'By taking people out of their traditional way of thinking, we got them to work together successfully. We were able to reduce our product development cycle, and our time to market, by 50 per cent. Our best competitor requires a couple of years to produce a new product, but we can do it in less than 12 months.'[2]

> 'Large FMCG companies have to contend with three major blocks to innovation that are ingrained in their structure and culture: size, hierarchy and corporate governance.'

However, it's not easy for a big traditional corporation with its rigid hierarchical structures to introduce many of these emancipating measures. Large FMCG companies have to contend with three major blocks to innovation that are ingrained in their structure and culture: size, hierarchy and corporate governance. In this chapter we'll look at the implications of these enduring problems and how they impact on another critical element of innovation – speed.

Most global FMCGs are still operating with organisational structures and principles based on a matrix system, which means that several management groups overlap, sharing accountabilities and responsibilities. When this happens in an organisation, it usually means that the clarity of command is clouded; it's often impossible to trace accountability for important decisions to a single individual.

The matrix structure has become very common. There is a staff dimension, where the head of a corporation's strategy tends to be the lead entity, and there

1   Sloane, P. (2010) 'Breaking down barriers to innovation', http://www.business-strategy-innovation.com/2010/04/breaking-down-internal-barriers-to.html (last accessed 5 December 2013).
2   Morgan Gould, R. (2002) 'Revolution at Oticon A/S: the spaghetti organization' (case study), IMD-4-0235, December.

is an operating dimension, in which the company's various businesses figure. The two sides of the matrix interact, with the staff dimension tending to be more heavily involved than the operating dimension early on in the direction-setting process, and vice versa later on, when the operating budget is discussed.

There are several arguments that support this form of structure, above all that it makes more efficient use of human resources and avoids potential cost duplications in staffing. It also enhances a co-operative culture. The major dysfunctional factor, of course, is that clarity of responsibility can become blurred, with no one being individually responsible for the performance of an organisational unit. Breakdown in culture can also be a high risk, involving confrontation, bureaucracy and frequent meetings, all factors that compromise the speed of an organisation. What's more, no one is fully responsible for his or her budget.

Let's look at how the matrix structure works in one major FMCG, Nestlé.

Nestlé has several businesses that are organised as free-standing entities, including Nespresso, reporting to the Senior Vice President (SVP) Strategy, who is a member of the board, and water, headed by an SVP who is also a member of the board. There are also businesses, like pet food, that operate autonomously within each of Nestlé's five geographic zones (Europe, America, Asia, Middle East and Africa).

However, the bulk of Nestlé's activities are organised through a matrix structure. Along the operating dimension the company is organised along five geographic zones and the key operating entities are the country organisations that manage the specific businesses. Along the strategic dimension, there is the SVP Strategy, to whom seven heads of business units report. The strategic dimension is heavily involved in setting the specific strategies for the various categories of business, with a global focus. The operating dimension is based on the annual budget for each operating unit.

'Matrix structures have a built-in ambiguity, with brand management at its core.'

This process seems to work well, not least because most of Nestlé's executives have been employed by Nestlé for several years, and job rotation regularly moves them from one dimension to another. Most are highly motivated to make the matrix structure work.

However, matrix structures have a built-in ambiguity, with brand management at its core. The brand team will be in charge of brand management, designing all the key elements of the mix – positioning, product, packaging, qualitative and quantitative support, pricing and so on. The brand results, as measured by market share, volume and profitability, are the brand team's responsibility. But the end-market management teams are also accountable for how the brand performs in their market, a tough deal for them when they have no say in deciding the key success drivers.

This built-in conflict between brand management and end-market management can be helpful in that the dialogue between the two simulates market conditions and reduces the risk of central brand management losing contact with real end-market consumers. But it can also stall activity and lead to market misalignment. Instead of the two teams facing the market challenges together, they end up accusing each other of lack of understanding and support. A typical example is relative price promotion – a source of never-ending debate. The end market would like to overcome a short term budget–value deficit (mainly end of quarter or year end) and would love to give a temporary price offer to the retailer and consumer. Central brand management, however, fears that these offers (especially if they are given in regular cycles) lead to the consumer constantly looking out for special offers on the brand, which can lead to long-term problems of image and value perception.

Other typical conflicts are with support programmes that don't fit with certain short-term needs with an end market. If the brand runs programmes in more than 100 markets some of them find the centrally developed programmes 'not right for our market'.

Then there's the issue of why a brand loses market share. If this happens to a matrix organisation there will be a lot of finger pointing because there are numerous people who can be held accountable. The centre will point out that certain centrally developed programmes or design updates have been working in prototype; the end-market management, on the other hand, will be quick to argue that the new design or promotion was less competitive – hence they lost market share.

Let's take a hypothetical example: in Norway, say, the market share of Acme washing powder drops, so the general manager in Norway will want to do something fast to regain market share. The simplest thing is to lower the price – we call this temporary price reduction, which is an elegant way of pretending that you have not really cut the price, you are just lowering it for a certain period of time. The centre will be up in arms about this, maintaining that price reduction in one market will affect the positioning of the whole brand. All of a sudden Acme washing powder will no longer be a premium product.

Another typical area of conflict is advertising. The centre devises a new campaign – television commercial, printed ad or similar – and the local markets will come up with many reasons why the campaign will not work where they are. The fact is that in matrix organisations there are two realities that are difficult to understand and reconcile because globalisation is still relatively young and we all grew up with the dynamics of an end market. Suddenly we find ourselves in multi-markets. If all the markets are added together, it gives you a new global construct, a new number: Acme washing powder, let's say, grew globally by three per cent last year. This may be true, but that number hides the fact that in Norway, and nine other markets, it declined by 20 per cent. How do you deal with this? It would be unfair for the ten underperforming markets to be criticised because the mix doesn't work where they are: what they need is a local response. So there are two realities: one is the aggregated reality, which the centre communicates to investors and the outside world; but equally valid is the multiple of the market. It is extremely difficult to balance both of these.

Within a matrix structure, this kind of conflict is inevitable. Even within marketing itself you can have conflicting interests where sales and brand marketing are discrete departments. However, here we are going to focus on the one area of conflict that is critical for innovation capability: marketing, R&D and end markets.

End markets are naturally geared to relatively short-term interests, such as how to make the numbers in a month, quarter or year. For people working in this department, delivering these results is the key performance indicator. In most cases, they are also operating to a personal timescale of typically three to five years until their next promotion or posting. As a result they will exert pressure to bring new innovations to the market faster, whether it is to perform better against the competition or to justify a price hike at the retailers.

However, as our discussion of the typical external supply chain in Chapter 4 showed, in a company that doesn't own this side of the value chain – and most don't – the end market can be a major hindrance to fast product innovation due to the extreme challenges of stock management and expensive and disruptive buy-backs of old stock. Hence the power of having your own stores in the mix, as companies like Apple, Nespresso and IKEA do.

'End-market management
hates ambiguity, especially
from headquarters.'

End-market management hates ambiguity, especially from headquarters. They want activities that are well defined and planned on an annual cycle and they want as long a lead-time as the supply chain and retail promotion cycles require. Securing a promotion with a big retail chain like Tesco or Wal Mart is very expensive, so annual, biennial or even longer cycles are more manageable, particular in the context of a global supply chain. The innovation gap that results from this is relatively unimportant for end markets, which would rather fight on price than mess up their cycle plans.

R&D has a very different agenda. This department measures itself on how many successful innovations it develops and if R&D is market focused, innovation will be measured by the ability to sell products successfully at a higher price. If not, innovation stops with the development of a strong product pipeline. Product development can be project-based, which fascinates R&D people, but sometimes has no real consumer need or relevance, such as solving a technical challenge that they have been working on for years but which is unimportant or even unrecognisable to the consumer.

Speed to market is of secondary importance for most R&D departments. They are more inclined to take pride in developing big, breakthrough product innovations as opposed to small features or upgrades. Their preference therefore tends towards operations that imply significant investment and lengthy time to market.

Finally, there is marketing management, whose top priority should ideally be the sustained success and growth in value of the brand. This doesn't mean that marketing can afford not to focus on short-term financial success, but the marketing department is the only

'Brand value, which ultimately
determines the value of the whole
company, is not measurable in ways
that can be represented on the
balance sheet or quarterly report.'

group in the organisation for whom value creation plays a critical role and is the pride of management. The issue is that brand value, which ultimately determines the value of the whole company, is not measurable in ways that can be represented on the balance sheet or quarterly report. And so we can see that internal organisational challenges ensure a constant struggle to balance what's right for the consumer, the sustained viability of the brand, the tactics of the marketplace and the annual financial plan.

The organisational challenges of switching to a new, faster innovation process are often too big to resolve without creating major upheavals in the business. So who should lead innovation within the organisation?

It is generally accepted that most people reach the peak of their creative abilities during their early thirties; but managers in their thirties usually have a young family and have a lot of financial responsibilities as well. This means they are usually highly motivated to secure their position and further their career prospects and so they are likely to play it safe, sit tight and try to please. Senior creatives at advertising agencies and design studios frequently contend that junior brand managers are the death of real ground-breaking ideas and that they are among the most conservative people in the organisational hierarchy. This hierarchy can comprise as many as eight layers, which is the reason why senior management sees often highly compromised ideas.

Senior managers in their mid-forties or early fifties, who have usually reached the pinnacle of their careers and cemented their position in the hierarchy, may be more prepared

> 'Who should lead innovation within the organisation? The people who should dare don't and those who would dare can't.'

to take risks but don't have the cutting-edge ideas to match their sang-froid and often have so little empathy with target consumers in their teens or twenties that their judgment is compromised. Most senior executives have grown up with a certain way of doing business and, more significantly, with a fixed idea of the archetypical consumer – usually based on the target consumer when the company was in its prime growth mode. And so the people who should dare don't and those who would dare can't.

Underlying all this is that performance is based primarily on criteria internal to the company, often with a heavy dose of political overtone.

Let's take an example.

John was picked out as a fast-track executive in the wealth management sector of a leading global bank, headquartered in Switzerland. He received training as a trader within different areas (stocks, bonds, currencies, agri-commodities and precious metals) and in the Americas, Asia, the Middle East and Europe. This training programme, with extensive rotations, took two years. Not only did John become familiar with most aspects of wealth management, but he also observed several changes among target customers: no longer accepting fixed fees, but preferring performance-based fees instead;

rejecting the bank's own bundled products in preference for unbundled assets that could be brought freely on various exchanges, and so on.

John was then head-hunted by another bank, and became a successful trader there with responsibility for several private investors' portfolios. But he ran into friction with his new employer. First, he refused to include the bank's own products in his portfolio, contrary to the orders of the bank, which made more money on these. Second, he criticised the bonuses awarded to senior management, which were calculated on the performance of the bank's own products, as well as from fixed fees. The end result was that John was fired – not for poor performance but because he did not conform to the hierarchical expectations. After some time, John returned to the bank where he started his career, but now needed to start out all over again and build a new client base. He had lost seven to ten years.

This scenario, which is all too common, might not have been so serious in the past when there was a certain degree of consumer stability. Today, however, with a rapidly changing and evolving consumer base, this kind of inward-looking approach can prove fatal to an organisation.

When the profile of the target consumer changes so radically and constantly, it presents a real dilemma for many corporations that find it hard to keep in touch. The new, emerging multi-tasking consumers, for example, are probably more easily understood by younger executives who are able to relate to them. But, in many organisations, it is the more traditional, senior executives who call the shots.

How do companies respond? One way might be that the executive cadre becomes younger and younger, while older executives increasingly find themselves parked in staff or advisory roles, or offered early retirement. In one way or another, the result is organisational stress.

Let's take another example.

A major fast-food consumer goods company had organised its operations into several zones, one of which was Europe. To understand its emerging customers better, the executive management in the zone was relatively young and executive meetings always had one main theme: how are key customers changing and what key innovations should be emphasised now. The performance of this young team was impressive: higher growth and a more solid bottom line than its major competitors – a dramatic shift from the lack of performance in the past. But the other side of the coin was the potential bottlenecks created by older, although very far from superannuated, executives at the centre who in many ways had become surplus to requirements.

Many young companies don't have this problem. Some are started by people in their twenties with no corporate experience. They are usually led by a small group, often the founders, who own a big share of the company and have a very flat, non-hierarchical structure. They live the dream and get away with it. Analysts judge these companies on revenue growth rather than all the other short-term profit-and-loss measures.

The best examples of this type of company could be seen at the peak of the internet bubble, when new companies achieved multi-billion dollar market capitalisation without any sign of profits in the near future. Many died a death, of course, but what they all had was an extremely innovatory and open structure with clear top-down decision making from the owner, coupled with extremely lean processes and a strong, young team spirit. Everybody wanted to work for them even if they paid a fraction of the salaries offered by investment banks.

Another example of extremely fast innovation is the big fashion labels that have to bring new products to the market at least twice a year. They are usually built around one single designer, or at most a small group of designers, who can bring fast innovations that get the consumer hooked. This type of innovation is not research based but depends on personal instinct and genius, the in-house designer very often being a global superstar in the world of fashion. It's clear that there is also a top-down command structure that doesn't have to pass through numerous hierarchical levels and filters. These designers create billions in value for their labels. And as a result designers like Tom Ford become as much a part of the brand as any other element because of their celebrity status. They build on this and in many cases go on to create their own brand. The replacement of these chief designers is the key sustainability issue for big fashion companies, for which succession should always be on the risk register.

Both of these examples demonstrate the crucial role of the leader in inspiring staff, demanding creativity and driving innovation. But relying on a charismatic leader brings its own problems. Everyone ages, people get ill – but what happens when that person is someone closely associated with the brand – like Apple's Steve Jobs, who died in October 2011, or John Galliano, fired by Dior earlier the same year following a public outburst of antisocial behaviour?

Dior found that Galliano was considered too tough an act to follow for its first choice replacement, Marc Jacobs, but eventually tempted Raf Simons away from Jil Sander. Galliano himself lay low for the best part of two years before returning to fashion with Oscar de la Renta at the New York fashion show in 2013.

Apple had had the experience of losing its iconic leaders once already.[3] In 1985, both Steve Wozniak and Steve Jobs left the company, Jobs resigning before he could be fired after falling out badly with John Scully, who had been brought in as CEO from Pepsi. Scully was a typical FMCG man and the antithesis of Jobs. He didn't fit either the brand or, more importantly, the corporate culture and, to cut a long story short, Jobs eventually had to ride back into the fold and rescue Apple, from which point, until his death on 2011, the company never looked back. Charismatic entrepreneurial leaders are the most difficult to replace; Jobs hoped to nurture and educate future leaders through the Apple University but immediately after his death, many commentators predicted a decline in Apple's standing and performance would soon be seen.

Sure enough, in April 2013 Apple reported its first year-on-year decline in earnings for almost a decade and its shares fell through the floor. Incredibly, the company whose by-word has been innovation since it began, seemed to have dropped into the innovation gap, as cheaper rival products started to catch up. Having set up expectations of six-monthly innovations among its loyal customers, and having reached the number one most valuable brand position in the global market in 2012, Apple was apparently being penalised by the general assumption that it was late delivering whatever its next offering might be. The non-appearance of another game-changing product six months after the launch of the iPhone 5 and iPad Mini – the point at which Apple shares reached an all-time high of $705.07 – prompted speculation that innovation had dried up at Apple. As a result, share value plummeted by 44 per cent in six months, a loss equivalent to the entire value of P&G or Google. Commentators indicated that Jobs's successor, Tim Cook, needed to reassure Apple's customers and the markets about forthcoming innovations and give some guidance about Apple's future, otherwise his own future at the company would be in danger.

> 'The cement that binds all creative and innovative organisations is top-down management driven by inspired and informed leadership.'

3   Isaacson, W. (2011) *Steve Jobs*, London: Little, Brown.

Despite the inherent risk, the cement that binds all creative and innovative organisations is top-down management driven by inspired and informed leadership. There needs to be somebody sitting high enough not only to take the long-term view but also to take in the entire vista. Strong top-down management enables an organisation to predict cycles, spot opportunities and develop something the consumer understands. Bottom-up management makes an organisation reactive rather than proactive and decision by committee simply slows everything down. A true leader creates more room for fast innovation and a better chance of taking advantage of cycles in innovation.

Typically, bottom-up management is driven territorially while top-down is driven by brand innovation. This poses a dilemma for most classic FMCG companies, which traditionally let ideas and recommendations flow up from the bottom to the top. This guarantees that all the organisational experience is captured and that there is a formal alignment process. For example, the brand manager has to present to the country manager, then the regional manager and so on up the chain, with each level being persuaded in turn to accept the idea. On the positive side, these different layers of bureaucracy serve as risk filters and there are benefits for individuals throughout the organisation to grow their talent through exposure to senior managers. But the process is messy, time-consuming and a built-in barrier to speed. It also promotes low-risk ideas and kills off the real breakthrough ideas very early on. FMCGs can't work with a radical top-down approach – too many layers would be obsolete if the top started telling everyone what to do. Ken Levy, Executive Director of Client Services at G2 Worldwide, shares his views on the marketing demands facing FMCGs from a creative's perspective:

> *For today's FMCG companies to acquire the speed, dexterity and broad global perspective required to innovate in today's global market, they need clarity all the way from the top of the organisation down to the end markets about who is in charge of decision making. Delays or misinformation are roadblocks to satisfied consumers and brand growth. In today's consumer conversation-driven marketplace, customers won't wait days for their discussion to advance. Online social communities will forge ahead and make their own-brand decisions – good or bad – if brands don't act quickly and join the dialogue with positive input. The feedback needs to be accurate, insightful and timely with virtually no sensitivity to country borders since the internet doesn't screen by boundaries. Even then, there is no guarantee that communities will accept the argument and, based on the conversation, the brand is likely to have to weigh in again. This is quite different from the more traditional way of working that we were used to just a couple of decades ago, where information was pushed and consumers were patient.*

Of course some organisations are better equipped to address the changing marketing dynamic than others and that is often dictated by the company's cultural heritage. Take P&G: from its founding in the nineteenth century it has always been consumer-focused and has displayed lots of traditional buccaneering American spirit – not altogether surprising given that it was established in a Midwestern town with basic Midwestern values. Up until recently, P&G was led by a graduate of the US Military Academy at West Point, Robert McDonald. You couldn't ask for a more old-fashioned legacy and yet McDonald's officer background, reinforcing the company's all-American spirit as well as the top-down 'follow me' hierarchy of decision making, actually suits the current global environment well.

While P&G grew out of its Cincinnati roots via acquisition (beginning with Thomas Hedley of Newcastle on Tyne in the UK in the 1930s and culminating in the huge global acquisition of Gillette in 2005) it has remained steadfastly a US-based company with the optimism and can-do attitudes that have driven America to much of its success. P&G is almost an analogue of America itself – a cultural melting pot which, despite many acquisitions across a broad number of categories, has remained true to its focus on brand management and its consumer-driven orientation. Acquired companies, brands and their people have either fitted into the P&G way of managing business or have moved on.

During its 1998 restructuring, in preparation for the new millennium, P&G again refocused on brands. Its plan, dubbed 'Organisation 2005', aimed to double revenue from $35 billion to $75 billion in less than ten years. A key shift was from a geographically oriented organisational structure established in 1995 to one centred on seven global business units, including beauty care, baby care, fabric and home care. The aim of this was to improve innovation and speed to market by focusing strategy and profit responsibility globally on brands rather than geography. This coincided with P&G's emphasis on creating billion-dollar brands, which forced decision making to be more vertical and consistent. Subsequently there was little debate across a brand on key strategic drivers and innovation. Local implementation might be different on a brand like the fabric softener Downy (Lenor) but there was no question that it would deliver 'superior softness, unique freshness and the ultimate in loving care for moms'. This message was delivered top-down and was accepted throughout the organisation.

P&G accepted that minor disagreements might take place within the structure but the centre (global HQ in Cincinnati) was in charge and the organisation would align accordingly. While local brand managers were proactive and engaged they would ultimately subordinate their point of view to the broader strategic parameters of the brand and well-circulated 'best practices'. Huge though it was, P&G pretty much felt like one company attitudinally, executively and vertically and its decision-making process was well articulated and adhered to. In this structured environment there were not many rebels.

P&G's big rival Unilever also dates back to the late 1800s, when Jurgen and Van den Berg opened their first margarine factory in the Netherlands. At about the same time, Lever and Company started making soap in England. Towards the end of the 1920s these two companies came together and Unilever was born.

This company has grown both organically and via acquisition and for much of its history Unilever was a true Dutch–UK company operating as two legal entities but with a common board. With this type of organisation it is easy to see how top-down decisions could occasionally become complex and how cultural integrity might be split by the mixed heritage and two-company operating model.

The first decade of the twenty-first century has proved to be a period of significant growth for Unilever, kicking off with the acquisition of Slim Fast and Ben & Jerry's Ice Cream in early 2000 and continuing up to the present day with acquisitions including the personal care division of Sara Lee. Equally importantly, under the leadership of Paul Polman (the first Unilever CEO to come from outside the company, having previously served as CEO of P&G Europe and CFO of Nestlé) Unilever has embarked on 'The Path to Growth' and implemented its 'One Unilever' programme to align the company behind a single strategy. Polman's appointment in 2009 followed a period during which Unilever had two CEOs: one from the UK, the other Dutch. The appointment of a single CEO had an immediate impact on speed of execution. For a company like Unilever with €46 billion plus in sales across 190 markets, this is important, given today's fast-moving marketing environment. Unilever's desire for a more unified corporate culture and a more coherent strategic global focus can only help meet the company's need for accelerated growth. The old two-company structure certainly hampered Unilever's ability to move quickly and gave rise to ongoing debates on product and strategy.

BAT is another global FMCG brand that has had to change its command structure to fit the new marketing environment of the twenty-first century. Originally formed as a joint venture in 1902 between the UK's Imperial Tobacco and the USA's American Tobacco Company, for trading purposes it quickly embarked on an aggressive expansion and acquisition path that resulted in strong operations in a significant number of markets around the world. In the 1990s, under CEO Martin Broughton, the company began to acquire key brand assets from rival tobacco companies including Lucky Strike, Pall Mall, Dunhill, Rothmans and, of course, Kent. The challenge BAT faced in addressing global brands in the 170-plus markets in which it operated was the fragmented way in which the company came together: lots of end markets acquired with a wide variety of different cultures – all with a fair amount of strength because the category can be highly profitable – and all with a multitude of local brands.

Other FMCGs would benefit from the kind of financial savvy shown by the BAT marketing people. They really understand pricing, costs, margin and other factors. But their challenge was to use this expertise to transform the company globally into a much more single-minded, strategically aligned organisation.

Despite strong leadership there were still divided loyalties. Managers were paid more on financial returns and overall market growth than on brand health and other key market factors. Local managers reported to end markets and regions as much as they reported to the centre. On top of this, while strategy could be aligned, actual implementation was limited by restrictions in the end markets due to legal constraints on reaching the target – for example, only certain types of communication were allowed in trying to reach 'of-age' smokers.

Two other factors further complicated the move to more single-minded strategic alignment and execution. First, BAT frequently moved its marketing people around – a normal tenure was 18 months. This is too short a time to create, execute and read big bold marketing moves and individual key performance could only be activated and measured over a short term. Second, BAT paid its agencies on a 'horizontal' basis so that end markets funded end-market agencies, regional agencies covered regions and the centre was paid by the global headquarters. And, of course, we all know that power follows money, so loyalties weren't vertical despite the desire of the corporation to be more aligned from top to bottom.

There was still too much of a gap between commercial needs, overall marketing goals and end market independence. All too often aggressive discussions would take place between the end market and the centre on the appropriate way to launch initiatives only to fall apart when marketing directors returned home to face the realities of growing volume. As much as the central team at the agency might push the agenda from the centre, end-market agencies – who were part of the same network as the central agencies – had the allegiance to the end markets that hired and fired them so they would do what the end-market client desired. This sometimes happened in a covert way without feedback to either the central client or agency team. Given the overall complexity of unique end markets, the huge revenue growth and profit returns the company was generating, few of these differences actually got back to the centre with enough impact or urgency to stimulate someone into making changes. The result was lots of short-term growth but a huge number of missed opportunities for further accelerating a brand's equity and long-term growth. Factors such as packaging architecture and key messages became sub-optimised globally in order to satisfy local end-market needs.

In an attempt to align the loyalties more locally, Jimmi Rembiszewski, then head of marketing at BAT, instituted a practice in which the agencies were invited to present ideas directly to him. This was more or less a political nightmare for any agency, leaving them very uncomfortable and exposed. For each agency, their client (worth the most money) was the local manager; but now the global head of function, more powerful but actually less valuable to the agency, was coming in and stirring things up. They didn't want to dump their client (the local brand manager) in it in front of the top guy. But Rembiszewski was confident they'd get over their discomfort in time and that the result would be more alignment of ideas. He always maintained direct contact with the key creatives and took care to build a relationship with the top people in the agency, who could call him directly (but hardly ever did). In practice, Rembiszewski corrupted the system and overrode decisions made by local brand managers. He exposed the agencies uncomfortably but made sure they considered him the ultimate client, not the market. In the long run, he clearly got it right: in a company that moved on its marketing people every 18 months, he remained as marketing director for nearly 20 years. But as he points out himself, this needed enormous trust on the part of BAT.

The hypothesis offered here is that a company's heritage has a significant impact on how the corporation operates. The cultural orientation of the management clearly impacts upon the speed and clarity with which brands are managed. This can range from the alignment of the more uniformly cultural P&G to the truly multicultural BAT. As we have seen, Unilever has reached outside for leadership and is becoming a more unified operation. These changes are all brought about by the realities of today's markets where geographical boundaries are tumbling down. In addition, reaching consumers to grow brands is now much more dependent on interaction – real engagement – with these users. Consequently, marketing organisations must be set up to be responsive and join conversations. They need to communicate from top-down and back as one. Being vertically oriented and quick is no longer something that's simply nice to have – it is mandatory.

One way for big organisations to deal with the sluggishness caused by size and lack of agility is to create a new company around an innovation – a company with its own profit-and-loss, management and infrastructure, down to new reward systems, on the principle that it is easier to spin something out than change the whole thing. These companies-within-companies can be designed from scratch to incubate innovations and look for radical new approaches.

Once again, a good example is Nespresso, whose success in a market context we looked at in an earlier chapter. Nespresso is a totally independent company from the old Nestlé organisation, and has its own management and new end-market units. It was set up as spin-off because it didn't fit the Nestlé

'One way out for big organisations to deal with the sluggishness caused by size and lack of agility is to create a new company around an innovation.'

mould – it required the input of 'different' (that is, entrepreneurial) people, not ideal in a big company environment, and it would not have worked as part of the parent company. Spinning off was the only way it could innovate and move fast. The venture was hugely expensive and the company was prepared to invest in its belief in the concept but it couldn't remodel the entire business along these lines.

It must have been a real challenge to get the finest talents into this small unit. But after more than two decades Nespresso became one of the most admired marketing moves of all time. Only because someone high in the organisation kept believing in this dream was it kept uncompromised and so successful. Nespresso had to be subsidised by the mother ship for decades until it turned a profit.

'Why be big if you can't turn size to your advantage any more?'

Family-owned and medium-sized firms can move faster than big FMCGs, which raises the question: why be big if you can't turn size to your advantage any more? The need for top-down innovation, the capacity to move fast, more integration in value chain – all these things run counter to what's being taught and implemented today in terms of positioning, brand, use of ad agencies and campaigns. And yet our observations of today's success stories indicate that it is the only way forward.

Within the largest companies, people become hung up on preservation. What happens when these companies get to the point where they simply stop innovating and try to optimise? They need to stick ruthlessly to the twenty-first century regiment of fast innovation cycles, even if that comes at a huge cost and major internal pressure from the finance people. That this is a real challenge can be best seen at Nespresso, which started life as a fantastic, twenty-first century innovation. However, in the past three years Nespresso has reverted to more traditional, old-fashioned marketing instruments, such as TV advertising and short-term promotions, and has created a big innovation gap with multiple low-price entries. One could speculate that the Clooney campaign marks the end of Nespresso's run of success.

Global versus Local Creativity

In the debate between top-down and bottom-up management, is neither totally right nor totally wrong. There is a very fine line to be drawn between the corporate genius and the corporate clown – only the results will tell you who is who. Some things, however, seem key to us: you have to keep control of the supply chain, the brand, the value chain and promotions. There are various ways of doing this, even within the largest organisations. Both designers and creatives have to be close to consumers. If consumers could say what they will want or need in a few years' time, life would be easy and bottom-up would work – but they don't know, or at the very least they can't articulate this, so we have to tell them.

With the dawn of the twenty-first century a new type of relationship between advertising agency and client started to emerge. It may have been in response to the lack of answers to the new consumer and marketing models,

> *'You have to keep control of the supply chain, the brand, the value chain and promotions.'*

or as a result of the enormous cost pressure the old FMCGs found themselves under, or both. It started with new contracts that moved away from the old model in which the client paid a commission of 15 per cent of media spending covering all agency costs in a dynamic way.

This model was based on the belief that the agency was a partner in the success and failure of the brands it worked on. If the client experienced growth or expected growth opportunities, it would spend more on media, so the agency got more. If the client was less convinced about a brand's ability to grow it would spend less and the agency would make less. Fifteen per cent was the norm, and allowed the agency to plan, grow top talent and come up with new initiatives that would entice the client to spend more. This was a healthy form of symbiosis, decoupled from cost or profits on both sides. The critical element was the health and growth prospects of the brand. The hard indicators for both client and agency were market share and certain attitude and usage parameters of the brand. The interests of both were exactly aligned. The agency would come up with all kind of proposals to ensure the brand would grow market share. These did not stop at advertising; they covered the whole marketing spectrum. The skills profile of the account manager had to match that of the brand manager to be successful in the long term. The annual budget process that determined the media spend – and the agency income – was a shared exercise. The agency had a say in the annual planning cycle both quantitatively and qualitatively. In today's world this sounds like a lost paradise.

Today the model is mostly cost-based, which means that the client pays the agency its costs, plus a margin, plus certain incentives that are negotiated on an annual basis. This move from brand investment to marketing cost has proved to be the death of a real partnership.

The client started to regard and treat the agency as a cost item, no different from raw materials or distribution. And as a consequence the client started to use the same procurement principles for the annual agency cost negotiations. Very little was left for a real breakthrough initiative on either side because of the fixed nature of the cost-based contract. In this new relationship the health of the brand was a soft item while the hard debate focused on costs.

Since most of the costs were people's salaries, the only way the agency would get its margins up was to get overheads down and scale up the side of their business where size mattered a lot, such as media buying and planning. As a first step they developed their own media departments, which became big profit centres. But with media spending slowing down and fierce competitive pressure from other media buyers and the stations themselves, plus the advent of new media, significant margin growth could only be achieved through consolidation of the agency landscape. As a consequence, we now see agency corporations that have gathered together numerous agency brands under one global umbrella. WPP and Publicis are the two largest publicly traded marketing services groups in the world and together they own world-class agencies including Y&R, Thompson, Saatchi and Saatchi, Grey, Ogilvy and Mather, Leo Burnett and many more. They brought financial discipline and used the new scale to bring costs down and improve margins by sharing certain services and combining media buying power.

The move to a cost-based relationship, together with the consolidation of the agency sector, effectively broke the sense of partnership and aligned purpose that had previously existed between agency and client and moved the focus away from the core common interest – the brand – to never-ending debates about cost. A tied cost framework agreement on both sides made new initiatives that were not pre-agreed in the annual budget almost impossible.

Success started to be measured in terms of compliance with the procurement process instead of the growth of the brand. As the agencies are under shareholder pressure themselves, hitting financial targets quickly becomes the key focus for the agency. When you ask your agency partners today, 'How is business?' they relate the question to their agency performance. But as a client what you really mean is, 'How is the brand you handle for me doing?' And that's what you want to hear.

Today a global client basically has only two agency groups to choose from – WPP and Publicis. This makes agency choice a commodity or a cost choice, as opposed to what it used to be – 'a creative programme' and a way of getting a competitive edge. There was no way that Unilever would put one of their brands with an agency that was associated with a competitor, Chinese walls or no Chinese walls. Choice of the agency partner used to be a competitive advantage and even the exchange of best practices was not permitted. It was quite natural to drop an agency that took on a new client that you perceived as a competitor, even if the agency was doing an excellent job. By working for another firm in the same sector, the agency was no longer giving you that competitive edge.

As a consequence of these cost-driven relationships, some clients add to their global agency support new, smaller boutique agencies that they hope will produce more breakthrough ideas. In some cases, consultants and even audit companies have moved into the marketing space and started taking over what agencies' account and strategy departments used to do.

Classic advertising agencies have lost their marketing skills because of the lack of human resources; their in-house training and recruitment has been reduced significantly through cost pressure.

The search for a new global agency client model is one of the key issues for the twenty-first century and our prediction is that in the next five to ten years we will see a new model emerging. The shift in agency revenue from above the line to below the line can be seen across the board. It has already resulted in agencies developing a new skill set: what may be called 'marketing services', focused on promotion, packaging, product, trade marketing and research.

Creating a global model for these new disciplines has proved much more complex than establishing global creative and media capabilities as it requires local expertise that a lot of global agencies do not carry. The current solution therefore is to produce product, pack design and advertising for use in multiple markets. This is predicated on the belief that there is convergence among young consumers – in other words, that the 18–25 age group is fairly constant around the globe: a 20-year-old from Japan would have more in common with someone in the same age group in France or the US than with a 60-year-old compatriot.

The spread of social media has acted as an extremely efficient catalyst for this trend and the result can be seen in any high street around the world: most shops, restaurants and night clubs look very similar everywhere and products and services are very homogeneous.

In most cases subtle adjustments are made to food products to meet local taste profiles. Even a product like Coke has a different taste in a lot of markets. Another driver for adjustments is differences in regulation and legislation. However, most of the elements of a global marketing strategy and its execution are standardised on a day-to-day basis.

In order to deliver these global cost synergies, companies have restructured their marketing organisations significantly. Instead of the central marketing department setting strategy for the local markets to execute, the new model has a centre that produces all the marketing mix elements, from which the local market builds its own vehicle for delivery, incorporating the necessary local adaptations.

To complement this, the agency networks have also centralised their organisation and moved their best creative talents to a central hub. Most of these central hubs mirror the global client and are set up in close proximity to their clients' headquarters. To facilitate acceptance in different markets, English – the undisputed international language of commerce – has became the default language and while this has obvious cost benefits (you produce one film, one slogan, one picture) this has severely reduced the scope for creative execution. In some industries, using English may be cool – in the way that American and British popular music has made the language cool in non-English speaking regions – but if you are not speaking to your customers in their native language, you do not have the same ability to exploit linguistic idioms, establish catchphrases and introduce subtle wordplay into your message.

A good example of this is BAT's Vogue brand of cigarettes, a brand with clear French connotations, as the name indicates. This brand was managed centrally from England, which happened to be the worldwide centre, and had English on all the packaging and support material. The character and style of Vogue obviously had to be French and so it was decided to develop a French marketing mix for the brand from London. This did not work. So instead the Vogue central creative team was relocated to Paris – and the outcome was fascinating. The design and indeed the whole marketing concept was soon outstanding and totally different from anything London would have been able to create. And although this was achieved at significant cost, and was more complicated than the fairly streamlined, centralised creative process, it was worth it.

Based on that experience, BAT then tried to establish different creative centres in places where it was thought the best and most differentiated creative talent for various brands would be found. The idea was to use local talent in the creative process towards a global concept. However, it proved difficult to get the right creative talent and the communication between these regional creative centres was poor. Furthermore, these initiatives were difficult to defend whenever the question of cost reduction was mooted. It is very difficult to make a business case for certain creative processes but very easy to make a business case for concentration of resources and sharing infrastructure costs.

Real consumer insight can only come from dialogue with local consumers and great marketing ideas are nearly always generated locally by creative people who can convert and adapt them. In the next few years we expect to see a trend towards 'create locally and expand globally', bringing back local creative boutiques that will compete for the best ideas within a global network. Competition and dialogue between local 'idea centres' can be managed much more cost-effectively with today's communication technology and even if it can't compete with the globally centralised process on cost, it will pay its way in great ideas.

In the end, good consumer business comes from competition between great ideas. Lower cost is a one-off benefit not suitable for a sustainable process like brand building on a global stage. So *vive la différence* between talents, cultures and ideas in the creative process, while the exploitation of these ideas and concepts can take full advantage of a well-designed, centralised global machine.

Corporate Governance, Habit and Caution

In the fallout from the global economic downturn, corporate governance has become as much about damage limitation as how the company is led and developed. It increasingly has the effect of taming wild ideas, a tendency that should be resisted. This is not the case with the top-down, dictatorial leadership characterised by Steve Jobs at Apple, and at the major design houses. At the Danish shipping company A.P. Møller-Maersk, Arnold Møller was CEO for 50 years and his son Maersk Mc-Kinney Møller for 52 years following him. At the age of 80, Maersk Mc-Kinney Møller decided he needed a CEO and stepped down from the post but remained on the board. His successor did not make a success of the job; poor asset management saw the company's shares drop. Sometimes you need a dictator.

'Creative people need the freedom to take risks and corporate risk management puts the brakes on their innovative activity.'

In brief, corporate governance slows things down. Creative people need the freedom to take risks and corporate risk management puts the brakes on their innovative activity.

Let's take a closer look at some of the impediments – habit, caution and vested interests – that might slow down innovation processes.

There has been an unprecedented level of development in materials science over the past few years but some of the industries that could benefit from it are failing to take advantage of its innovative potential. One of the leading materials science experts in the world, Professor Jan-Anders Månsson of EPFL in Lausanne, Switzerland, claims that most of the innovations in his field can traced back to two main benefits: better aero/fluid dynamics and the development of lighter and stiffer materials.

And Månsson knows what he is talking about. After all, he was one of the main forces behind the Swiss twice-winner of the Americas Cup with monohulls (2003 and 2007). Månsson maintains that this type of innovation only takes place in fields where there is a strong sense of urgency. For many years he was a professor at the University of Seattle and a consultant to Boeing. He campaigned forcefully for the introduction of more composites-based, lightweight, added-strength materials in the design of commercial planes. But there was a lot of resistance from the large cadres of design engineers who were trained to use aluminum. In addition to having to retrain themselves – developing new know-how and discarding some of the old – they also had to testify that such new designs would be entirely safe. But why take the risk? Innovations were not adopted thanks to a combination of conservatism and concern for safety; in other words, excessive risk aversion. It should be pointed out that in the new Dreamliner, which has since been introduced commercially, there is extensive use of composites-based materials – in fact as much as 55 per cent. But this innovation was made a commercial reality a good ten years after Månsson campaigned for their use.

After Boeing, Månsson turned his attention to the automotive industry, particularly family car manufacturers. Cars could be made lighter, stronger and safer using various types of composites, as indeed they have been. But here, too, there was strong resistance to rapid adoption, especially from the supply chain: heavy investment had been made in assembly plants to produce parts and cars made using more traditional materials. The cost of switching to new materials would simply be too high, at least for an immediate conversion. And, why risk massive recalls – with both heavy costs and loss of brand reputation –

by introducing untried innovations? Månsson estimated that his innovations might take around five years or so before adaptation in the automotive world.

Finally, Månsson turned his attention to the world of sports – pole-vaulting, ice hockey, skiing, cycling, swimming and so on – all of which require some sort of equipment. Here the quest to improved performance was undisputed and immediate: how can I set new records and win *now*? Lighter bicycles, more flexible ice-hockey sticks, stiffer skis for jumping – they were all developed through the innovative uses of composites. Even new swimsuits were developed using these materials to achieve better aqua-dynamics and less friction.

These innovations were adopted almost immediately, reflecting the immediate need for better performance. In this field there were few if any constraints imposed by fear of risk or conservative thinking. In fact, this went so far in modern sports that concerns for safety and fairness had to be established through legislation – spearheaded mostly through international sports federations and the International Olympic Committee (IOC). For example, various types of bike design and ultra-light materials were banned. Minimum requirements for stability and brake capacity were introduced. Similarly in swimming many of the new swimsuits types were banned for reasons of fairness in the competitions.

Innovation works very differently in a more cost-driven sector. Seaspan owns modern container ships that are chartered out to various container lines, much as aircraft leasing companies provide planes for airlines. Between July 2008 and July 2011 the cost of a ton of bunker fuel went up over 300 per cent from $60 to $200. Economic considerations at customer level – the container lines – called for more fuel-efficient ships, new designs that would incorporate innovations for a more fuel-efficient performance.

However, coming up with a new ship design requires co-operation from others, above all shipyards and ship classification societies. As long as their order books are healthy, shipyards generally want to build more of what they're good at – conventional types of ship. The longer the series of standardised ship designs, the more money they make. Long new-building backlogs are a function of the cycles in the shipping markets. But timing is everything: when freight expectations are low, the pool of orders for new ships diminishes, and even disappears. At this point in the cycle, the shipyards are hungry for new business and receptive to the introduction of new designs. If customers' requirements for innovation are strong enough, the yards' investments in old-style, heavy, steel-based manufacturing in long series will have to yield.

A similar argument can be made for ship engine manufacture. New fuel injection systems, through innovations in modern electronics, allow ships to run at lower speeds without causing damage to their engines. Classification agencies can also having potentially decisive impacts on the speed of innovation. For them safety is paramount. But this might also lead to excessive conservatism. They see no need to take the risk of being seen to endorse an innovation and see no reason to go through the hassle of explaining why a particular innovation is safe. It is easier to stick to the old standards.

Seaspan's response was to devise a specification for a new type of 10,000 20-foot equivalent unit container ship, with a fuel-saving capacity of as much as 35 per cent, which could maintain a similar speed to the existing fleet, typically 21 knots. Different Chinese and Korean shipyards developed competing designs, which were more water-dynamically optimal and tank tested. Lighter materials, including composites and aluminium alloys, were used, especially in the superstructure. Det norske Veritas (DnV), the ship classification agency, worked closely with Seaspan on this. The result was an immense weight reduction, which meant that more cargo could be carried for pay. A new generation of ships' engines was developed by MAK/Burmeister & Wain which also allowed for significant fuel savings, and additional slow steaming flexibility, primarily through a novel fuel injection system. Finally, better underwater coating to reduce friction, using epoxy-based technology, was developed by the paint manufacturer Jotun.

The customers' needs – in this case, significantly more fuel-efficient vessels – were the key driver for innovation for Seaspan. And so pressing were these needs in the face of rapidly rising fuel prices that production-driven standardised designs, cost saving through long ship series by the yards and conventional calls for safety-motivated conservatism by the classification agencies, were all overruled. Furthermore the cumulative effect of several relatively small innovations produced a significant innovation and top-down leadership from a great orchestrator – Peter Curtis at Seaspan – drove the initiative through.[4]

Another shipping case reveals what happens when resistance to change is stronger. The innovative ship design consultants Shipsteknisk in Ålesund, Norway, developed a new design for special-purpose ships to carry live salmon from fish farms to processing plants. Much of the initial process was supported

4   Lorange, P. (2013) 'Innovations at Seaspan' (case study), Lorange Institute of Business, Zurich.

by Peter Lorange's shipping company, S. Ugelstad. The innovation lay in the shape of the transporting tanks: round rather than rectangular.

The classic design for live salmon carriers is to have long, squared-off closed tanks, with oxygen pumped in at the fore end, where the bulk of the salmon would naturally congregate in a densely-packed mass. The result: delivery of stressed salmon to the processing plant, and reduced quality of the fish. Salmon are directional fish. Round tanks allow the salmon to swim in a circle, against a flow of water, and oxygen is injected at many places. This simulates the salmon's natural river habitat. The result: relaxed and happy salmon are delivered to the processing plant, important for optimal taste and quality. An additional bonus was equipping the ship with gas turbines to minimise the CO_2 footprint, a key factor for the transportation of food.

It sounds like a perfect solution, with welfare, environmental and economic benefits. However, only one ship was built. It was just not possible to make long-term chartering agreements with the major salmon-carrying ship-owning companies, nor with any of the well-established salmon farming and processing firms. Why? Because the new generation of salmon carriers would probably lead to the economic obsolescence of conventional equipment well before the end of its service life. So the players in the industry – ship owners as well as fish farmers and processors – resisted. Innovation is frequently resisted by actors who have invested heavily in conventional equipment.

We saw in the Seaspan example that a real innovation took place by building on several smaller innovations; and we saw how important it was that customers' needs and priorities drove the innovation. Let us

'Innovation is frequently resisted by actors who have invested heavily in conventional equipment.'

now consider an example from the automotive industry, to shed further light on customer-driven innovations within networks. When Sergio Marchionne took over as President and CEO of Fiat in 2004, the company was in trouble. The R&D department had not succeeded in coming up with innovations that its customers appreciated. Marchionne decided to relaunch the Fiat 500, which had been discontinued more than 15 years earlier. And he challenged prospective customers via the internet and social media to let him know what the key features of a relaunched Fiat 500 should be. He was deluged with suggestions, from which the new Fiat 500 emerged, without much input from the firm's traditional R&D community. And we all know the end result – a stunning commercial success.

Many of us, with good reason, associate Porsche with cutting-edge technology and most of us assume that a large, sophisticated corporate R&D organisation is behind it. Not so. Much of the ground-breaking research is done in universities by graduate students. It is, of course, orchestrated by the relatively small innovative R&D team at Porsche, but the key is that graduate students are closer to the real users. So what can we learn from this? Once again, we learn that when it comes to innovation the customer is key. The closer we can get to the customer, the better. Innovations, not necessarily large but of the type that the customer can understand and attach value to, are critical when it comes to customers' purchasing decisions. So, relevant innovations rather than lower prices are a crucial driver.

Nokia provides us with a cautionary tale. A decade ago, in 2002, Nokia had 60 per cent market share in mobile telephony; today it has about 18 per cent. The company fell off a cliff. What went wrong? Quite simply, it missed out on the smart phone due to its own big-headedness as market leader and its disastrous separation from the consumer. It's a hard lesson in how, nowadays, the creation and destruction of thousands of billions of dollars can take place in less than five years. Fifty years ago, the capital of a brand was estimated at between 120 and 150 years. Now it's 10 years. Before, if a company made a mistake, customer loyalty to the brand would get it through; today, if a company misses an innovation cycle, it's finished. Nokia, Eriksson, Kodak and Phillips, once the leaders in all their sectors, are all now second-rate companies because of this. Eriksson's story is typical. The company had had huge success with mobile telephony systems masts, switches and associated infrastructure. Then, 25 years ago, the head of Eriksson Radio piloted an idea for a handheld computer that could take photos, process text and make phone calls. Everyone thought he was crazy and the initiative was halted by the head of Eriksson, a man who in his time had pioneered big-deal electronics for telecommunications. The field was left wide open for Apple.

Our final example is the Lorange Institute of Business Zurich, a small graduate business school on a beautiful lakeside site in Switzerland. The Lorange Institute aims to be a leader of a change process within a generally rather conservative industry. Innovations have taken several forms since the institute's inception in 2009. Unlike many leading business schools, the Lorange Institute does not employ permanent faculty, preferring to draw on a stable network of leading management scholars and practitioners from around the world. Participants in courses keep their full-time jobs while studying at the Institute. This requires modular programmes and a more intensive learning methodology. Administration and support are largely outsourced to networked suppliers, reducing bureaucracy within the Institute and improving speed and adaptability.[5]

All business schools want accreditation from the three leading agencies that help regulate business school activity: AACSB (Tampa, Florida), AMBA (London) and EFMD (Brussels). But new approaches within an accepted model and breaks from traditional, well-established methods create a dilemma for accreditation agencies. They have to strike a balance between insisting on the fulfilment of quality standards that have been established over time and the recognition of untried innovations that aim for improvement. This can be particularly difficult, given the need both to safeguard quality and stimulate innovation. In practice there may be a bias towards the former – that is, stick to what works – which also eliminates the need to explain why such-and-such an innovation has been approved. In this way, accreditation agencies can actually delay innovations, and weaken quality over time, rather than enhance it. It is a similar dilemma to the one faced by ship classification agencies. To date, the Lorange Institute has received accreditation from AMBA and EFMD.

Four key criteria stand out when it comes to successful innovation. The first is proximity to customers – we saw a prime example in the CEO of Fiat who reached out to customers and ensured that their desires, beliefs and requirements were designed into the new Fiat 500. The second is that those customer requirements will be the driver of innovations and implementation, as our examples from the very different fields of car and aircraft manufacturing and sports technology demonstrated for the field of applied materials science. The third, illustrated by the revolution in container ship design, is the cumulative impact of several smaller, networked innovations. Finally, we saw the importance of an integrator, someone who would put various smaller innovations together – 'assemble' the bits and pieces – to achieve a significant innovation. The orchestrator is often critical to the successful implementation of innovations.

These four criteria for success are balanced by four major factors that can delay, or even kill off, innovation. The first is resistance among people who might be expected to be natural adopters of an innovation because of the implications for their current asset holdings. We saw this in the live salmon carrier case. The major ship owners would have faced the almost complete obsolescence of their existing fleets if the new design had been adopted.

5   Thomas, H., Lorange, P. and Sheth, J. (2011) *The Business School in the Twenty-first Century*, Cambridge: Cambridge University Press.

At Seaspan many of its existing container vessels would become economically obsolete long before the end of their technical life as a result of new ship design. However, the benefits of the new design outweighed the cost of accelerated obsolescence. While automotive companies resisted innovation because of the expensive traditional manufacturing capacity already installed, the shipyards agreed to change from building traditionally designed container ships to going for the new design.

The second is legitimate concerns such as safety and quality, which were illustrated in our examples of aircraft manufacture, ship classification and academic accreditation. These must, of course, be adhered to – but we need to take care that they are not used systematically as excuses for not considering innovations or as reasons for blocking them.

> *'Conservatism and conventionalism, supported by agencies, can bring innovation to a standstill.'*

The third is playing it safe. Why change something that seems to work or is good enough already? Conservatism and conventionalism, supported by agencies (ship classification, academic accreditation bodies), can bring innovation to a standstill. We saw an example of this in the stillborn early Eriksson smart phone. There must be some sort of dialogue between the 'old traditional' and the 'new innovative' – some vehicle to bring this tension to the surface. Fourth and finally, legislation can be the kiss of death to innovation, as we saw with the materials science-driven innovations in sports.

Getting support for our products or services by incorporating innovations that customers see as relevant and useful is a formidable task but it can be done, as the examples above show, despite some imposing barriers to innovation. Imagination, determination, persistence and speed are crucial.

Conclusion

Ingredients – But No Recipes for Success

Given the complexities of the problems facing FMCGs in the new millennium, this is a rich field for exploration, but we believe that other authors have proved to be less intuitive and more categorical than us.

Two recent publications essentially defend the established notion of brand management and innovations as extensions of what has previously been set in motion. In *Playing to Win*,[1] the authors set forth an elaborate approach to systematic brand management, using P&G as an example. The approach smacks of excessive formality and excessively complex patterns of analytical interdependencies and interactions among specialist groups. We are left with the impression that this might be more 'inside-out', that is, the existing organisational entity rationalising how to do things, rather than 'outside-in', when key actions stem from the modern consumer. And what space is there for speed and flexibility amid all this complexity and organisational silos? In today's world, 'playing to win' calls for speed and flexibility, empowering creative individuals, and openness to new business models, rather than bureaucratic, one-best-way approaches.

The second book, *Strategic Transformation: Changing While Winning*,[2] also deals with how to come up with new, winning business models, based on in-depth analysis of eight leading corporations. The authors conclude that successful transformation is based on one or more traditions: continuity, anticipation, contestation and mobility. Surprisingly, there is no reference to the changes represented by the modern consumer, but as we have argued throughout this book, we believe that there has been a dramatic shift here, even a discontinuity. Neither do the authors discuss communication and the need for innovation.

1   Lafley, A.G. and Martin, R.L. (2013) *Playing to Win: How Strategy Really Works*, Cambridge, MA, Harvard Business Review Press.
2   Hensmans, M., Johnson, G. and Yip, G. (2013) *Strategic Transformation: Changing While Winning*, Palgrave Macmillan.

Closer to our findings is Hermann Simon's *Hidden Champions of the 21st Century*,[3] which identifies a large number of small to medium-sized companies around the world that have become highly successful, even market leaders. The author attributes their success to their propensity to work closely with core consumers and to their ability to come up with innovations that the customer appreciates. However, there are three significant distinctions between our findings and those of Simon. First, he sees no discontinuity in consumer values between the immediate past and today and fails to identify young, web-based multi-taskers as a new, leading consumer group. Second, Simon's study included for the most part technology and manufacturing-based companies, in contrast to the FMCGs with which we are concerned. Finally, he does not make a clear link between the modern consumer, modern communications and innovations, treating them as more or less independent of each other, while we see these as inextricably linked and consumer-led. Nevertheless, Simon's research adds support to our findings.

In 2011, a Deloitte Research report described FMCGs as facing 'a crisis of the similar'.[4] Many of the challenges that the authors of that article identified resonate with the dilemmas we have described in this book.

The main problem facing FMCGs is one of product similarity and differentiation. Walk down any high street in any major town or city in the developed world and you are guaranteed to see the same stores with the same things in them. Today it's possible to navigate your way around a foreign city following a retail trail: if LK Bennett's here, Zara can't be far away. Looking for the Apple Store? Head for Orange or T-Mobile. And what do you find in those stores? A lot of the same thing, the result of never-ending product extensions and irrelevant innovations, improvements to which consumers are largely indifferent. The market is crammed with look-alike products and such poor brand differentiation that no single brand stands out. Worse, consumers perceive only negligible differences between branded and generic products. Differentiation has given way to variety, which increases scope for choice. But what is going to entice the consumer faced with shelves full of very similar products?

3   Simon, H. (2009) *Hidden Champions of the 21st Century: the Success Strategies of Unknown World Market Leaders*, London, Springer.
4   Conroy, P., Narula, A. and Ramalingam, S. (2012) 'A crisis of the similar.' Deloitte University Press, http://www.deloitte.com/us/4694135925862310VgnVCM2000001b56f00aRCRD.htm (last accessed 3 March 2012).

Similarity in product content and packaging is often matched by similarities in growth strategies, investment patterns, expectations of consumers' needs and behaviour and business model. Growth still focuses on netting new geographical markets and introducing new products or extending a range of existing products, which is also where most investments are made. There is a failure to understand the way modern consumers make purchasing decisions, where the real value of what they are selling lies, and the way they use the new social networking media to inform their choices. FMCGs are too often locked into retrospective relationships with both their customers and their suppliers, slow to change their ways of working and too departmentalised to be able to mobilise the agility needed to respond to changes in the market. They are too customer and focus-group led. This can be handicapping, as Henry Ford acknowledged in his famous quote: 'If I'd asked the customers what they wanted, they'd have said "a faster horse".' What is needed sometimes is discontinuous innovation, a leap of the imagination.

A second major problem is pointless innovation – never-ending product extensions and tweaks to products and their packaging, more often than not things to which the customer is totally indifferent, doesn't want or resents having to pay more for. The hard truth is that customers typically do not value the time spent on developing small incremental improvements and are not necessarily willing to pay for them. Adding a new enzyme to a washing lozenge that will keep clothes fresh for 48 hours doesn't do it for them – at least, not enough to stop them buying a less expensive competing brand or a much cheaper own-brand product. Few people's clothes get really filthy nowadays and the savvy consumer reckons that the cheaper imitative brands typically can do the job just as well. Incremental innovations do not make products stand out. And slashing margins to bring prices down to match own brands is just temporary displacement for slashing the company's own throat.

So what's the solution? As we have emphasised throughout this book, FMCGs need to innovate where innovation really counts. This means starting with the consumer and aligning products with consumer needs; having a value proposition that is clearly differentiated from the competition; targeting specialised products towards smaller, specific segments of the market and identifying overlooked consumer groups; speeding up the route to market; and looking outside their traditional comfort zone to other industry sectors to see what they are doing.

The kinds of innovations consumers look for today are either related to performance, convenience or desirability, or evoke emotional responses. Companies either have to match what consumers want or offer them things they had no idea they wanted but suddenly can't do without – we've seen several examples of these in this book. The fashion industry is an excellent model for this, as is the example of sports good manufacturer Adidas. These industries predict, meet and set trends. It isn't always necessary to think big either: if a small segment of the market likes something but a much larger segment doesn't, you can play on this to increase the product's desirability and image as a niche product only appreciated by the initiated. For example, the yeast-based spread Marmite is marketed with a 'you either love it or hate it' theme; and Pot Noodle leveraged public perception of its down-market qualities in a notorious and very popular TV campaign advertising it as the 'slag of all snacks', until the ads were banned.

Think Innovation

In this book, we have argued for marketing-led innovation: keep an external focus; look outside the sector; build a close relationship with agencies; be aware of reputational risk. The key words are 'think innovation' and marketers could do worse than to start with themselves. You have to be prepared to innovate yourself if you are expecting everyone around you to innovate. If you want your brand people to stay poised on the cutting edge, you have to make sure your own-brand image remains relevant. Jimmi Rembiszewski recounts that during his 20 years as Marketing Director at BAT he refurbished his office every three years, not merely updating the technology but completely redecorating and refurnishing the room, which was already the biggest and best in the building. His reason was basically the need to 'walk the talk': if your company's message is that it is equipped for change and innovation, it has to be seen to be so. If your people are hunkered down behind cubicles or making do with outmoded furniture and equipment, you are telling the world that you are stuck in the past. The board might have grumbled about the cost, not least when Jimmi's office was redone more often than the boardroom, but the expense was justified. The Marketing Director's office was a window display for the company. Some companies go further: the fourth floor at Nestlé's Vevey headquarters is a product exhibition centre, while Adidas has a 12,500 square metre Brand Centre at its headquarters in Germany.

The grand gesture is not always necessary, however. A strong visual statement about an organisation's philosophy can be made relatively simply.

When Peter Lorange bought a failing business school on the shore of Lake Zurich in July 2009, and renamed it the Lorange Institute of Business Zurich, one of the first things he did was announce that he wouldn't have an office. Instead he moved in a large captain's table – highly fitting for someone with his ship-owning heritage – and established it as his desk in the main entrance to the school. This was a very direct statement of his determination to transmit a major culture change within the organisation. The accent was to be on accessibility, transparency and openness. This undramatic physical reminder of the new Institute's message caused considerable discomfort. The undemonstrative Swiss did not take to it at first; in fact, they actively disliked it. But Lorange persisted: he had to find the antidote to the toxic culture he had inherited when he took over the school. The keynote of the previous regime had been control; people were expecting to follow orders. But Lorange wanted to push them out of that mindset, believing that a leader should encourage people to think any way they like and be accessible to them and their ideas. He sees this as the royal road to gaining competitive advantage. Today Lorange and his fellow executives work at the table and anyone can use it as a hot desk while visiting or studying at the Institute.

This same philosophy informs the culture of Beghelli, Italy's leading manufacturer of emergency lighting. The company was founded by Gian Pietro Beghelli in 1982 and enjoys a 50 per cent market share. It has been estimated that a quarter of Italian families have at least one Beghelli product at home – a remarkable statistic in a country where global brand awareness is very strong. Beghelli's businesses include domestic and industrial electronic security systems, consumer lighting, photovoltaic energy systems and personal emergency alarm systems for the elderly, the *Salvavita Beghelli* (Beghelli Lifesaver).

Beghelli's career started modestly, distributing components for Ducati. He quickly discovered he could make some of these components himself and enlisted his mother and others to make them at home. However, it was an emergency in his hometown of Monteveglio, in northeast Italy in 1976, that inspired him to start his own company. A snowstorm cut off electricity to the town. Beghelli recycled some Chinese light bulbs he had to hand, added some electronics and managed to get the lighting working again.

Today, Beghelli's annual turnover is nearly €150 million and the group has companies in the Czech Republic, Germany and Canada, as well as in Italy: centres for emergency and general lighting, electrical circuits, lighting components, and R&D, which receives an annual investment of 4.7 per cent of revenues and five per cent of sales. There are 1,660 employees worldwide, 150 of whom work in R&D. The company is family-owned.

One of Beghelli's key products is the Immediately Dual brand of light bulb, which incorporates a halogen lamp into an energy-saving bulb. The halogen lamp comes on automatically when the light is switched on but stays on only for the time it takes for the fluorescent bulbs to achieve the maximum light intensity. The halogen component then automatically switches itself off. In this way the bulb unites the advantages of a traditional incandescent bulb that lights up immediately with the advantages of an energy-saving class A bulb. This makes the product ideal for use in hazardous areas where instant light is needed (like stairwells). Better still, the bulbs have a potential lifespan of 10,000 hours – up to ten years.

In this family business, it is evident that the owner provides clear top-down leadership. Gian Pietro Beghelli ascribes the company's success to its strengths in R&D, innovation, distribution and communication. Innovations are indispensable as they constitute the only way Beghelli can compete with giants like Philips and Osram. Although many innovations may seem incremental, they respond to needs and can be done at low cost. Beghelli never make copycat products. Some innovation is in design because Gian Pietro Beghelli believes people appreciate good design, especially in the overlooked industrial applications market. He generates many of the idea himself, as does R&D. So how does innovation take place in Beghelli?

The founder asks around for people's opinions about his ideas. For example, he might discuss an idea for a consumer product while playing pool at the local bar. If he is thinking about an industrial application, he will refer it to his staff of electricians. However, the key is speed to implementation. If Beghelli believes in an idea, he makes up his mind about it in *three minutes*. He believes this style of decision making is a competitive advantage.

To Sum Up

Multi-tasking modern consumers appreciate innovations that are centred on developing new versions of the prestige products and services they see as 'must-haves' and that are available when they want them. Speed is critical, hence many relatively small business-led innovations seem to be more effective than large, path-breaking innovations spearheaded by a central R&D department.

It then becomes essential to communicate these innovations effectively to consumers through the media they understand, like the web and social networking sites.

We claim that when these processes work as intended, companies can count on selling more (top-line growth) at a higher price (better margins, bottom-line growth).

Innovations also tend to create new business opportunities, often for new players at the expense of established ones. The best-known recent example of this is the way the Apple iPhone and Samsung Galaxy have knocked Nokia off its predominant position in the mobile phone business. Nokia fought back with advertising and lower prices, but in vain.

It is critical to look for sources of resistance to innovation. For companies that have invested heavily in plant, materials and expertise, innovations in production methods and technology may pose a huge financial challenge and can make earlier inventions (potentially) obsolete. When Seaspan first tried to build the new container ships we read about in Chapter 5, it met determined resistance from the shipyards, for whom it was more lucrative to continue to build ships to conventional designs, where all the bugs in the construction process had been eliminated over time. Only when their order books fell, due to the depressed shipping market, were the yards willing to innovate – in order to survive.

This raises the question of how to deal with obsolete inventory and systems. Owning your own stores, like Apple and IKEA, means that new generations of products can be introduced rapidly; independent distributors, conversely, risk finding themselves stuck with outdated items and having to discount heavily. Outdated, of course, does not necessarily mean useless – witness all the relatively new container ships, technologically fine but economically obsolete, that are now being ousted by the triple-E new builds. A further challenge for many large companies is how to accelerate depreciation to keep pace with accelerated rates of change.

In this book, we have discussed how to reach the new consumer from a practical point of view. A key point is that today's modern marketing should centre on a plan of the innovation steps to be aimed for and a plan for communicating them. Together this might call for a new business model for a route-to-market. But everything starts with understanding the consumer and consumer needs, which we maintain must be driven by the line rather than a specialised department.

The twenty-first century has significantly altered the corporate landscape and brought new stars to the fore. Today we see corporations and brands that did not exist 20 years ago dominating the top global ratings. They have made it from good to great – but they are not the household names of the last century that Jim Collins identified in his famous book of the same name. That list is now populated by new giants such as Apple, Facebook, Google, Samsung and Starbucks, which have not only benefited from the rise of the new consumer but have also established new business models externally as well as internally.

P&G, Unilever, Colgate and Nestlé – the FMCG giants – have to recognise that these global brands are real competitors because they have been more successful in the contest for the twenty-first century consumers' disposable income.

Throughout this book, we have identified some of the major factors that drive brands and illustrated some of them with reference to specific companies: marketing strategy (BAT), reliable products and services (Lego, Nespresso), process innovation (Zara) and leadership (Apple, A.P. Møller-Maersk). Other factors include corporate culture – attracting and retaining employees; 'best places' to work (like Facebook and Nike, which feature on most 'best places' lists); product innovation or constant product improvement (L'Oréal); control of sourcing and distribution (Coca-Cola); network externalities – creating loyalty and raising switching costs (Microsoft); and unique brand intangibles (Disney 'magic').

Nobody disputes that the right innovation builds brands. But without fast innovation, brands will die. To compete better for the modern consumer it is critical to move from being an old-fashioned FMCG to being an FICG – a fast *innovating* consumer goods company. This implies being able to cut innovation cycles from, say, six years to six months. Furthermore, new marketing strategies are needed. The modern consumer is no longer attracted by single-minded, predictable and one-benefit-focused brand promises. The old-fashioned communication strategies based on television, radio and print with constant repetition has become outdated. These strategies must be replaced by what we call 'Lego' strategies, whereby the marketing and communication strategies are built up by many key facets (like Lego blocks) and delivered to the consumer through a mix of various touch-points. Most importantly, you need to leave consumers to put it all together themselves.

There are major internal and external hurdles to being successful in transforming FMCGs into FICGs. It requires new brand strategies and flatter, more top-down than bottom-up, decision-making organisations and a twenty-first-century model for advertising agencies. Externally these companies need a new route to market through transformation of their old retail dependencies. Changes are also required in all communication delivery, reflecting modern consumers' connectivity and unlimited access to information.

We cannot give a comprehensive solution to the issues at hand, but in this book we have tried to point out what the winners of the twenty-first century have in common that has enabled them to move from good to great. As we progress into the third millennium, we are sure that new, as yet unforeseeable, models will emerge. We can also be sure that the habit of discounting as a result of the innovation gap is not sustainable for any consumer goods company, nor for the retail trade. Both need to find significant responses to the twenty-first-century consumer.

Bibliography

Allison, M. (2006) 'Starbucks takes unique approach to marketing', *The Seattle Times*, 12 October.

Armstrong, L. (2011) 'Tom Ford: "I'm probably the only man in England who doesn't want to dress in drag"', *The Daily Telegraph*, 7 September.

Baker, R. (2011) 'Kraft leverages Cadbury brand for Oreos in India', *Marketing Week*, 5 July.

Baldwin, C., Hienerth, C. and von Hippel, E. (2006) 'How user innovations become commercial products: a theoretical investigation and case study'. Harvard Business School Working Paper 06 032.

BBC News, 27 November 1998, www.news.bbbc.co.uk.

Black, L., Kay, H. and Faith, N. (1993) 'Runaway consumers put heat on brands: "Marlboro Friday" has been seen as a health warning for many companies with heavily promoted product names', *The Independent*, 25 July.

Breillat, A. 'You Can't Innovate Like Apple', www.pragmaticmarketing.com, accessed 19 February 2014.

Bryson, B. (2007) *The Life and Times of the Thunderbolt Kid*, London, Black Swan (Transworld), pp. 105–9.

Campbell, C. (2004) 'I Shop therefore I Know that I Am', in Ekström, K.M. and Brembeck, H. (eds), *Elusive Consumption*, Berg, New York.

Cartwright, L. (2011) 'iPad cads scalping buyers', *New York Post*, March 16.

Chandon, P., Bart, Y., Sweldens, S. and Seabra de Sousa, R. 'Renova Toilet Paper: Avant-garde Marketing in a Commoditized Category', INSEAD, Ref 510-077-1.

Chasser, A. and Wolfe, J. (2011) 'Brands rewired', *IAM Magazine: Brands in the Boardroom*.

Clark, A. (2011) 'Rise of the Apple iPad puts Apple within touching distance of the biggest brands', *The Times*, 5 October.

CNN.com (2001) 'Zara, a Spanish success story', 15 June.

Cohen, P. (2011) 'Innovation far removed from the lab', *The New York Times*, 9 February.

Collins, J. (2001) *Good to Great: Why Some Companies Make the Leap… and Others Don't*, New York, Random House.

Conroy, P., Narula, A. and Ramalingam, S. (2012) 'A crisis of the similar.' Deloitte University Press, http://www.deloitte.com/us/4694135925862310Vg nVCM2000001b56f00aRCRD.htm (accessed 3 March 2012).

Crook, C. (2011) 'Apple After Jobs', *The Atlantic*, 25 August.

The Daily Mail (2011) 'Has Marlboro man had his day? Philip Morris to market aerosol that gives a nicotine hit without the need for cigarettes', 27 May.

Davies, P.J. (2013) 'Banking's handy revolution', *Financial Times*, 28 February.

Dediu, H. (2011) 'At $2.9bn/yr apps are challenging songs as the most valuable online medium', www.asymco.com, 6 October.

Digital Trends (2009) 'Digital Blue teams with Lego', 12 January.

The Economist (2013) 'Dr Seldon, I presume', 23 February, p. 68.

Edgar, R. (2009) 'Burberry looks to win over friends online', *Financial Times*, 26 September.

Felicias, L. (ed) (2011) *Trend-Marke Nespresso: Der Schweizer Kapsel-Boom*, FastBook Publishing.

Fernandez, J. (2010) 'Cadbury and the amazing chocolate brain drain', *MarketingWeek*, 21 July.

girven.com (2008) 'Human Brands: Tom Ford and Tom Ford', 16 November.

Gordon, R. (2012) 'Is US Growth Over? Faltering Innovations Confront the Six Headwinds', working paper 18315, National Bureau of Economic Research, Cambridge MA.

Green, P. (2006) 'This Season's Must-Have: The Little Black Roll', *New York Times*, 18 May.

The Guardian (2013) 'Tesco expected to scrap struggling US grocery chain Fresh & Easy', 12 April.

Hansen, S. (2012) 'How Zara Grew Into the World's Largest Fashion Retailer', *New York Times*, 9 November.

Hensmans, M., Johnson, G. and Yip, G. (2013) *Strategic Transformation: Changing While Winning*, Palgrave Macmillan.

Hienerth, C., Jensen, M.B. and von Hippel, E. (2011) 'Innovation as consumption: Analysis of consumers' innovation efficiency', MIT Sloan School of Management Working Paper.

House, M. (2008) 'How Marlboro Friday Changed the World', The Motley Fool (www.fool.com), 15 January.

Hume, M. (2011) 'The secrets of Zara's success', *The Daily Telegraph*, 22 June.

International Herald Tribune (2012) 'How fast is too fast in fashion? The rapid rate of growth at Zara's parent risks the sustainability of its model', 9 November.

Interbrand, www.interbrand.com.

Isaacson, W. (2011) *Steve Jobs*, London: Little, Brown.

Joseph L. Rotman School of Management, University of Toronto, 'The Starbucks Brand', Rotman Case Series (no date or author name supplied).

Kamprad, I. (1976) *The Testament of a Furniture Dealer*, Inter IKEA Systems, Delft.

Kaplan, R.S. and Norton, D.P. (1996) *The Balanced Scorecard*, Harvard Business School Press.

Kashani, K. and Miller, J. (2003) 'Innovation and Renovation: the Nespresso Story' (case study), IMD–5–0543, December.

Kaufman, R. 'Education Makes Starbucks' Customer Service Quality Star Shine', www.upyourservice.com, accessed 18 February 2014.

Kets de Vries, M.F.R. and Simmons, S. (2007) 'Envy me? The Rise and Fall of Gucci', INSEAD Case 06/2007–5447.

Knowledge@Wharton (2011) 'The Bitter and the Sweet: How Five Companies Competed to Bring Chocolate to China', 12 January.

Lafley, A.G. and Martin, R.L. (2013) *Playing to Win: How Strategy Really Works*, Cambridge, MA, Harvard Business Review Press.

Lefebvre, D. (2010) *Nestlé Nespresso: enabling the growth of the world's leading coffee producer*, Lockwood Trade Journal Co., Inc.

Lefevre, A.S. (2013) 'Pepsi suddenly scarce in Thailand after bottler break-up', Reuters, 22 February.

Lehrer, J. (2011) 'Steve Jobs: "Technology Alone Is Not Enough"', *New Yorker*, October 7.

Lorange, P. (2013) 'Innovations at Seaspan' (case study), Lorange Institute of Business, Zurich.

Malik, O. (2009) 'How Big Is the Apple iPhone App Economy? The Answer Might Surprise You', *Gigaom*, 27 August.

Metro (2013) 'Tesco confirms US exit as annual profits fall', 17 April.

Morgan Gould, R. (2002) 'Revolution at Oticon A/S: the spaghetti organization' (case study), IMD-4-0235, December.

Morris, B. (2008) 'Steve Jobs speaks out', *Fortune*, 7 March.

Music Ally (2011) 'Apps catching up to songs in value for Apple', www. musically.com, 7 October (accessed 20 February 2014).

Nash, E. (1999). 'The discreet mogul fashioning an empire', *The Independent*, 27 October.

Negus-Fancey, C. (2011) 'There's no such thing as an original good idea', *Huffington Post*, 6 October.

Negus-Fancey, C. (2011) '"Badvocates" and advocacy marketing', *Huffington Post*, 7 November.

Neild, B. (2011) 'How Net-a-Porter uses journalism to sell fashion', *globalpost*, 1 March.

Parise, S., Guinan, P.J. and Weinberg, B.D. (2008) 'The secrets of marketing in a Web 2.0 World', *Wall Street Journal*, 15 December.

Pfanner, E. (2009) 'Once Wary of the Web, Luxury Brands Embrace It', *New York Times*, 18 November.

Reuters (2011) 'Q&A – What happens to Apple after Jobs?', 6 October.

Russell, H. (2013) 'Lego school promises the building blocks to successful learning', *The Guardian*, 22 April.

Russollilo, S. (2013) 'Apple loses throne as world's biggest company', *Wall Street Journal*, 17 April.

Ryan, O. (2001) 'Spain's retail success story', BBC News, 23 May.

Shepherd, R. (2011) 'Net-a-Porter.com tries augmented reality on for size', *Computing*, 8 September.

Simon, H. (2009) *Hidden Champions of the 21st Century: the Success Strategies of Unknown World Market Leaders*, London, Springer.

Sloane, P. (2010) 'Breaking down barriers to innovation', http://www.business-strategy-innovation.com/2010/04/breaking-down-internal-barriers-to.html (accessed 5 December 2013).

Smith, S. (2010) 'Is Kraft killing the goose that lays the golden eggs?', *Marketing Week*, 6 November.

Tarnovskaya, V.V. and de Chernatory, L. (2011) 'Internalizing a brand across cultures: the case of IKEA', *International Journal of Retail and Distribution Management*, 39 (8), pp. 598–618.

Thomas, H., Lorange, P. and Sheth, J. (2011) *The Business School in the Twenty-first Century*, Cambridge: Cambridge University Press.

The Times, 5 October 2011, p. 43.

Torekull, B. (2009) *Slik gjorde jeg det! Eventyret Ingvar Kamprad – mannen som pakket verden flat,* Publicom.

Tonkall, B. (2006) *Historien om IKEA*, Walström and Widstrand, Stockholm.

Turner, C. (2010) 'The future of the Cadbury brand revealed', utalkmarketing. com, 3 February.

Wilson, D. (2010) 'F.D.A. Seeks Explanation of Marlboro Marketing', *The New York Times*, 17 June.

Wiseman, E. (2010) 'One-click wonder: the rise of Net-a-Porter', *The Observer*, 11 July.

Index